BEDFORDSHIRE CASEBOOK

A reinvestigation into murders
and other crimes

Paul Heslop

The
Book
Castle

To the memory of my parents

By the same author

The Job — 30 Years a Cop

The Walking Detective

Old Murders and Crimes of Northumberland and Tyne & Wear

First published November 2004 by
The Book Castle
12 Church Street
Dunstable
Bedfordshire LU5 4RU

ISBN 1 903747 57 0

Designed and typeset by Caroline and Roger Hiller
The Old Chapel Graphic Design

Printed in Great Britain by Cromwell Press, Trowbridge, Wiltshire

Foreword

Ian Whinnett

In his deliberations the modern detective is faced with a series of possibilities, some of which can be confirmed by scientific fact. Others, often the result of a hunch, can only be assembled, then fairly and skilfully placed before a jury for consideration. Analysis of historical cases is a fascinating pastime, provided one is equipped with the appropriate guide.

Paul Heslop is well qualified to present accounts of these varied crimes, which will provoke interest and debate far beyond the county of Bedfordshire. As a police officer, Paul was open-minded and deep thinking, yet persistent and meticulous. This lively, extremely well researched book takes the reader way back to crimes, investigations and trials of long ago, as well as some more recent cases.

It will enlighten, amuse, intrigue and surprise. You will, however, be encouraged to reach your own conclusions.

Ian Whinnett served for over 30 years in the Hertfordshire Constabulary, rising to Detective Superintendent. In this capacity he was responsible for the investigation of crime throughout that county, as well as targeting major criminals as Branch Commander in the Regional Crime Squad over an area covering the northern Home Counties and Bedfordshire. Many of his cases were high profile, including investigations into murders which invariably led to a successful conclusion. He is more than qualified to judge the merits of Paul Heslop's book, itself a journey of reinvestigation into similar crimes.

The Author

Paul Heslop is a former policeman who served in two police forces, Newcastle upon Tyne City Police (later Northumbria) and Hertfordshire Constabulary. He joined the Newcastle force in 1965, in the days when coppering was done on foot, supervised by patrol sergeants and inspectors, and on the street contact with the public was seen as an essential ingredient in policing.

In a career spanning over 30 years Paul served in CID, Special Branch and Regional Crime Squads in both forces, as well as uniform duties. As a detective he was directly involved in the investigation of murder and other crimes. As detective inspector at Watford, Hertfordshire, he had operational responsibility for investigation into serious crime: murder and suspicious deaths, robbery, rape and sexual offences, child abuse and domestic violence, as well as routine offences. His regional crime squad work throughout the northern Home Counties included the investigation of suspected criminals in Bedfordshire, as a result of which he became acquainted with the county.

Since his retirement from the force in 1995 Paul has established himself as a successful writer. His autobiography, an account of a walk the length of the country and a book on 'old crimes in the North East' have been published. His work for newspapers and magazines includes such diverse topics as crime, local history and walking, and health and safety features. He is an ardent fellwalker and climber of Scotland's mountains. He lives in the Lake District.

Contents

And naked to the hangman's noose
The morning clocks will ring
A neck God made for other use
Than strangling in a string.

A.E. Housman

I

WRESTLINGWORTH 1843

"Unequalled in the annals of crime"

The Sarah Dazley Poisoning Case

'It is my duty to pass the awful sentence of law upon you, that you be taken from this place to the gaol from whence you came and that you be hanged by the neck until you be dead, and that your body be buried within the precincts of the gaol in which you shall be confined after your conviction, and may God have mercy upon your soul.' Thus did Justice Baron Alderson sentence Sarah Dazley to death in the time-accustomed way, solemnly advising her to look for mercy, not from any earthly tribunal, he said, but to her Redeemer. 'I am not guilty,' she declared, before being taken down, as they say.

In 19th century England, there was nothing unusual about these events, except that before passing sentence Justice Alderson had broken down in tears. And that, before uttering the final, damning words to the 28-year-old woman in the dock, in a place where he might from time to time have found the need to call for 'order', he was out of order himself, for as well as sentencing Sarah Dazley for the murder for which she stood convicted, he condemned her also for murdering her child, for which she had not been tried and convicted.

The murder for which Sarah had been sentenced was of her second husband, William Dazley, who had died by arsenic poisoning.

1

So had Sarah's child by her first husband, Jonas Mead. It was suspected that Sarah's first husband, Simeon Mead, had been poisoned too, but this was never proved. As far as the demands of the law were concerned, one conviction was enough. You can only hang once.

It was 1842, and with two husbands and her son dead and buried, young Sarah was due to be married for a third time, to George Waldock, a farm labourer. The banns had been read when George pulled the plug. A woman friend told him, 'Surely you are not going to marry that she-devil,' pointing out the unsubstantiated fact that Sarah had already allegedly murdered two husbands and her baby. Unsubstantiated perhaps, but it was enough for George to call it a day. It was gossip, of course. But over four months after William Dazley's death, Police Constable Forester, who heard the rumours like everyone else, told the Chairman of the Quarter Sessions, who in turn instructed the coroner, Ezra Eagles, to hold an inquest on the death of William Dazley. The wheels of justice were in motion. The coroner fixed the inquest for Monday, 20th March, and ordered the body to be exhumed from Wrestlingworth churchyard.

Sarah Dazley fled. Not the actions of an innocent, you might think, but in those days, with your neck likely to be stretched if you were convicted of murder, who could blame her? She was arrested by Constable Gynn, in London. 'I know they say I murdered my husband,' said Sarah, 'but they can't prove that I bought the poison or gave him anything.' What a reply — they hadn't even examined the body. She might have been condemned on those words alone, if she said them, except that her defence may have been that she'd heard the rumours like everyone else.

Supt Blunden saw her after her arrest. She told him, 'I was on my way to Bedford to give myself up. I am innocent.' She appeared before the Lord Mayor of London (a procedure differing from today). Supt Blunden told the court that Sarah had left Wrestlingworth and he required authority to detain her and take her

The Dazleys' Cottage, Wrestlingworth

to Bedford. He was asked if there was a warrant. There was, said the officer, but not in his possession. You should have it with you, he was told. Well, he hadn't, he replied, for he had come in haste.

The procedural spat between the Lord Mayor and the police superintendent over, the latter said it was reported that Sarah had murdered her first husband and child with poison. She was married to her first husband six years, and to her second two years and nineteen days. The child was ten months old when he died. She admitted she was Sarah Dazley, which was just about the only thing she did admit throughout the entire judicial proceedings. 'I came to London to look for a situation because the parish refused to do anything for me,' she declared. The Lord Mayor said he would 'give her up' to the custody of Superintendent Blunden. Sarah said she had no objection! She was taken to Bedford, via Biggleswade, where she stayed overnight at an inn in the custody of two women who were obliged to sleep with her. They reported that 'the miserable creature cried all night'.

That Friday, Sarah was brought to Wrestlingworth, where she attended the adjourned inquest at the Chequers Inn. Witnesses were called to give evidence appertaining to the death of William Dazley. After hearing their testimony, the jury were treated to the gruesome details of the examination of William Dazley's body parts by George Dixon Hedley, surgeon. These were that when Hedley opened the stomach of the deceased man, two and a half ounces of 'dirty brown fluid' escaped. This was poured into a glass measure, and a white powder subsided at the bottom. There was more white powder on the surface of the stomach. The gullet was opened. More fluid and blood escaped, revealing still more white powder.

Hedley boiled some of the particles of the white powder in distilled water and added a few drops of the solution of ammoniacal nitrate of silver. This precipitated a yellow colour. To a second portion he added a little of the ammoniacal sulphate of copper, which caused green precipitate. A third, small portion was introduced, with distilled water, sulphuric acid and a piece of zinc, and the gas formed by this was set on fire, with a piece of plate glass held over the flame. The tests proved that the white powder was white arsenic. 'Are you of the opinion there was enough to cause death?' asked the coroner. 'I have no doubt,' said Hedley. The verdict of the jury was clear, that 'William Dazley died from the effects of arsenic administered to him with guilty knowledge by Sarah Dazley'. She was committed to Bedford for trial. They had accused her of murder. Now they had to prove it.

Sarah Dazley was born in 1819. Her father was Philip Reynolds, the village barber at Potton. He got lucky when his father left him a fortune, which he squandered through unsuccessful speculation. Unable to discharge his debts, he ended up in Bedford prison. Sarah visited her father there, without knowing that in time she too would

The Chequers Inn
Scene of the Inquest into the Death of William Dazley

be incarcerated behind bars in that very place. In 1826, when her father died, her mother remarried. But both before and after widowhood Mrs Reynolds was believed to entertain men friends, even in the family home. All in all, Sarah did not have the best upbringing.

In 1838, at the age of 19, Sarah married Simeon Mead, a local man. He was 20 years old. They were married at St Mary's Church, Potton and moved to nearby Tadlow, in Cambridgeshire, where they had a son, Jonas. In June, 1840, Simeon was suddenly taken ill, suffering violent sickness and pains in the throat. He died soon afterwards. Jonas died that November. Father and son were buried in Tadlow churchyard.

Not surprisingly, the neighbours rallied round Sarah, offering

St Mary's Church, Potton
Where Sarah Dazley married her first husband, Simeon Mead

support for a woman widowed, and having just lost her baby. She was not alone long, for she was soon in a relationship with William Dazley, whom she married in February, 1841. They moved to Wrestlingworth, so Sarah was once again ensconced in her native county. William was 23, a labourer. Sarah was still just 22 years old. At her insistence, Ann Mead, Simeon's 14-year-old sister, came to live with them. 'Marry in haste, repent at your leisure' is a common enough phrase, and one which might be applied to the marriage of William and Sarah, for soon after tying the knot it was apparent that things were not right between them. William would drink alone in the nearby Chequers Inn, and they were seen having a raging quarrel which ended up by him assaulting her. A few days later he was dead.

One Saturday in October William Dazley took ill. Mr Sandel, of Potton, was called, and prescribed medicine, which seemed to help recovery. But the following Wednesday, he was sick again after taking a pill which had been placed on a table by his wife. This caused

William to be sick into a cup, the contents of which were disposed of in the yard outside and evidently eaten by a pig. It was found dead the next morning. William seemed to recover again, and by the weekend he was almost back to normal. On the Saturday evening, after being given medicine by his wife, he became ill again and died on Sunday morning.

Mr Sandel requested permission from Sarah Dazley to do a post mortem examination. She refused. This was an astonishing state of affairs by today's standards — a suspect refusing an examination for evidence in the event of suspected foul play. And so William Dazley, a young man in his prime who had died so suddenly and mysteriously, was buried in the churchyard at Wrestlingworth. But fate decreed that things would not rest there.

Rumours filtered, gossip thrived. Two husbands and a child, all healthy people, all dead. Is it any wonder George Waldock cancelled the wedding arrangements? When Dazley's mother, Elizabeth, visited Keziah Mead, Simeon's mother, they lamented their lost sons. Elizabeth remarked that she had no doubt they had both been poisoned. 'Poisoned?' replied the shocked Mrs Mead. 'I know Sarah gave your son some quicksilver among some sliced onion,' said Mrs Dazley. Why didn't she tell the police?

Having exhumed William Dazley, they set about digging up Simeon Mead and his son, Jonas. On 20th April they opened two more inquests at the Chequers Inn. Simeon had died in June, 1840, Jonas in November of that year. Hannah Darts said that Simeon had complained of 'great pains' in the throat and mouth. Elizabeth Dazley corroborated this, adding that she had seen Simeon and Sarah quarrelling over a shilling she'd had, and he knocked her down and took it. Sarah said, 'Damn him, I'll poison him. I'll get rid of him.' Simeon Mead had complained of pains to his mother and his sister, Betsy, who said she'd often heard Sarah and her husband quarrelling, and that Sarah wished him dead. Why Elizabeth, Keziah and Betsy Mead kept silent isn't known. Maybe they considered it normal for

7

someone to threaten to kill a spouse or child — and, let's face it, it can be, even if it isn't meant — or maybe they just didn't know what to do about Sarah's threats.

George Dixon Hedley was again tasked with examining the remains of a suspected poisoning victim. But this time, when Simeon Mead's coffin lid was removed, he found only skeletal remains. Alas, nothing remained of the stomach or bowels. There was some 'soft black matter' lying on the bottom of the coffin, some remnants of a shirt to which were attached fragments of skin, and some remains of the front of the belly were found dry and partly converted into *adipocere* (fatty, waxy substance, resulting from decomposition), suggesting the grave was in a very damp place. Today, perhaps, modern technology would enable a scientist to examine the remains for traces of arsenic. Hedley was obliged to report that there was no evidence to show cause of death.

The child, Jonas, was under twelve months old when he died. At the inquest Sarah Morley, a local woman, said she had seen him on the Monday before his death, when Sarah had brought him to her cottage saying he was very ill. She left him with her to go into Potton 'to see Mr Spratt', to see if he could give her anything for him. She returned two hours later, saying she had three powders, and took Jonas home. An hour and a half later the boy was dead. Hedley, examining Jonas' remains, found the body decomposed but with parts of the belly in a 'tolerably good state' of preservation. He found metallic arsenic present. The jury decided that Jonas Mead 'died from arsenic administered to him with guilty knowledge by his mother, Sarah Dazley'. Local feeling rose angrily against Sarah Dazley. It was as well for her that she was locked up.

In July, 1843, Sarah Dazley stood trial at Bedford assizes, charged with the murder of William Dazley, her second husband. She was not indicted for murdering her son, Jonas Mead. It meant that evidence of both murders would not be heard, thereby weakening the case. Justice Alderson presided, and Sarah pleaded not guilty. Evidence in

Tadlow – Church and Churchyard

those days lacked the scientific analysis of today's criminal trials, but safe to say William Dazley had died through arsenic poisoning. But administered by whom? And why? His wife was the obvious suspect. One by one the witnesses testified.

Elizabeth Dazley said she was sent for on Sunday, 23rd October, 1842, to find her son ill in bed, 'very sick and vomiting'. Mr Sandel came about 4 p.m., and had a bottle of medicine sent to the patient. Elizabeth stayed with him until evening, then returned the next morning, and again on the Tuesday and Wednesday mornings when he seemed a little better. But on Wednesday he vomited and complained of 'heat' in his throat. She laid a bran poultice on his stomach, and put three leeches on his throat to draw blood. He vomited into a pot, which was emptied on to the front yard among straw. Next morning Mr Gurry's pig was dead. In the early hours of Sunday Elizabeth was sent for and saw him with his hand on his chest, vomiting again. He died in her presence about half past six that morning. At the time of his death several persons were present: Elizabeth, her husband, her two sons, John and Gilbert, Mr and Mrs Gurry and Mary Bull.

Ann Mead, sister of Sarah's first husband, Simeon, said she was 15 and had lived in the same house as the Dazleys until the Wednesday before William died. She had seen Sarah making pills in a saucer, which she wrapped in a piece of newspaper and put into her pocket. Sarah said she was going to Potton. She returned with some pills in a red box. She told William to take the pills, which she put onto the table by his bed. There were three pills, which appeared to be white. William said he could not take them, so Ann said, 'See me take one,' which she did. William then took one pill. That was at noon. About 2 p.m. Ann was sick and had a sore throat. She was ill for two or three days. She had the same symptoms as William Dazley. What happened to the third pill she didn't know. Ann Mead had knocked at death's door, for surely the one pill she swallowed contained arsenic, not enough to kill but enough to make her sick.

Mary Carver knew Sarah well, and accompanied her to Mr Sandel's on the Wednesday morning. Sarah asked for some pills for her husband but she was told, 'William must take his medicine.' He prescribed three 'resting pills' (made from opium). On the way back to Wrestlingworth Sarah took the pills out of the box and threw them into a ditch, then took the piece of newspaper from her pocket and put three pills from it into the box. 'They will do him more good,' she said, saying she had got them from Mrs Gurry. Mary Carver and Sarah parted company before they reached the Dazley house. Later Mary saw William to be 'wonderfully retching'. Under cross examination, Mary Carver said George Waldock had courted her the previous year, but (to laughter) said she didn't want to marry him. The defence were seeking to suggest she was testifying against Sarah out of jealousy.

Mr Sandel said William Dazley had complained of pains in the stomach, sickness and retching, all symptoms of a common irritation of the stomach. He treated him accordingly. He was surprised at his death, so much so he asked Mrs Dazley if he could examine the body. She refused. Mr Sandel said he did not keep arsenic in powder, and seldom put any white powder into 'resting pills'. He'd wanted to 'open the body to enlighten him as to the cause of death'. He had no power to do so (today a post mortem must be held when no death certificate is issued).

William Dazley's two brothers, John and Gilbert, gave conflicting evidence. John said he saw Sarah put some white powder, which she took out of a paper at the bedside, into a cup. She put some water in and stirred it with a spoon. William drank it at her request. He vomited blood. He said the scene was candle-lit (this was in 1842, when houses were gloomy and ill-lit). Gilbert, his brother, said he saw Sarah give William white powder, which was wrapped in paper, but that he saw her 'take it from her bosom' and put the powder into the cup, then pour water from a teapot into the cup. Clearly a discrepancy.

Other witnesses confirmed the presence of powder and pills. Even Mr Gurry, owner of the unfortunate pig, gave evidence. He'd found the pig sickly, so he put it into a barn where it died. It was only young, he said. Then came the damning evidence of Mr Burnham, the chemist at Potton. Damning because Mr Burnham recalled Sarah buying a pennyworth of arsenic 'about the fall of last year' – when William Dazley had died. Robert Norman, a boy employed by a Mr Bond, of Potton, recalled Sarah buying arsenic between ten and eleven months before 'to poison mice and rats'. This was a common enough practice then.

John Healey said he had seen William and Sarah fighting, even striking blows at each other. Then came the testimony of the two women who had stayed with Sarah at The Eagle, Biggleswade, after her arrest. They were Mary Ann Knibbs and Fanny Simmons. Knibbs slept with Sarah that night, at the behest of the police escort.

She said Sarah told her that the story about her throwing the pills into the hedge, as related by Mary Carver, was untrue. Sarah had said, 'They don't hang people as much as they used to.' Fanny Simmons corroborated her.

Hedley, the surgeon, said he had found at least one dram of arsenic in the body of William Dazley, more than enough to cause death. He described the symptoms of arsenic poisoning: vomiting, pain, tightness in the throat, faintness, more vomiting — exactly those of William Dazley. Arsenic in small doses is not 'thrown up' by vomiting; it is retained in the body. There was arsenic present in every test he made. He would not expect the victim to live more than two or three days 'after the contents of the bowels had escaped into the cavity'.

William Dazley had been murdered. But was Sarah Dazley his killer? Whatever the truth, she was not allowed to tell it, for in those Victorian days an accused charged with murder was not permitted to testify under oath, as it was presumed that anyone in such a position was bound to say anything to escape conviction. This monstrous rule must mean Sarah Dazley could not have had a fair trial. It is indefensible that someone accused cannot speak in one's own defence.

Defence counsel called no witnesses; all the relevant parties had been called by the prosecution. The jury was urged to ignore the rumours and gossip that had all but convicted Sarah Dazley before she stood in the dock. As to the testimony of Mary Ann Knibbs and Fanny Simmons, Sarah also told them, 'I cannot be hanged, because they cannot show that I either bought or administered the poison.' Did she mean she had not administered it, or that she had but they couldn't prove it?

In Sarah's defence, when her husband had taken ill had she not sent for the doctor, and more than once? Would she really administer poison in the presence of his two brothers? There were lots of friends and neighbours present at one time or another during

William's illness. As to the alleged purchase of the arsenic from Mr Burnham, he had no record of the sale. She denied throwing pills into a hedge. And even if she had administered arsenic, could it not have been by mistake, taken from somewhere in that gloomy house in the belief it was something else?

Where was the motive? What reason would she have had to murder her husband? There was no suggestion of another man. There was no money to inherit. As to her refusal to allow Mr Sandel to 'open the body', wouldn't anyone? If Mr Sandel had such concern, why didn't he tell the coroner? Defence counsel said that if she had committed the crime she must have gone through it with 'a quietness, a composure, a firmness and presence of mind unequalled in the annals of crime'.

What he did not say — well, he wouldn't — was that it was suspicious that her first husband had died young in similar circumstances to her second, and that in between, her son, not yet a year old, had been poisoned. No arsenic had been found in the remains of Simeon Mead, but it had not been possible to find any. It could not be proved that he was murdered, but equally it could not be proved that he was not. 'You must look for the truth,' the judge told the jury. Within half an hour they found Sarah Dazley guilty of murdering her husband. The judge broke into tears, 'completely overcome'. Sarah said, simply, 'I am not guilty.'

They hanged Sarah Dazley on 5th August, 1843, at Bedford prison. The hangman was William Calcraft, a man favoured of the 'short drop' and in consequence he often botched the job, leaving the condemned alive and thrashing wildly for life at the end of the rope. It is recorded that Sarah Dazley died quickly. Hangings were public events then, and it is reported that 12,000 people saw Sarah die. Thousands more gathered in Bedford, getting drunk and taking the opportunity to make a day of it. Others, convicted of the ultimate crime, confessed in their death-cell or even on the gallows. Sarah Dazley maintained her innocence until the end.

The Verdict

Sarah Dazley's son, Jonas, and her second husband, William, were murdered by means of poisoning. But was their killer Sarah? Surely she was, even though evidence of the murder of her baby was not given at her trial. If Sarah Dazley had murdered her husband and no-one else she would still have been convicted. Or would she?

Rumour, gossip, predetermined opinion by those in a small community had Sarah Dazley halfway to conviction before she stood in the dock. The jury would have known about the death of her first husband and the murder of her baby. Even the judge was prejudiced. Justice might have been better served if Sarah Dazley, charged with one crime only, had faced a jury in a far-off part of the country, where she and her background were unknown.

Lots of people came and departed the Dazley household when William was ill. Any one of them could have administered poison. But one by one they pointed the finger at Sarah. She lived with her husband; so did Ann Mead, but would she really have taken a pill with the words, 'See me take one', to persuade William to do the same, knowing it contained arsenic? The comings and goings took place after William became ill because he was ill — Sarah was already on the poisoning trail. She was seen to throw pills into a hedge, to wrap others in newspaper and substitute them for those prescribed. The evidence was overwhelming. It might have been fairer if she had been allowed to testify, if we could have known what she might have said under cross-examination. Who knows, she might have admitted the crime.

A Natural Turn for Poisoning

'Women have a natural turn for poisoning, usually by arsenic.' Thus reported the *Daily News* in 1873, alluding to the case of another woman poisoner, Mary Ann Cotton, of County Durham, who allegedly murdered about fourteen people, including four husbands, her children and even her mother, and possibly as many as 21. In saying so, the newspaper may have been taking into account the murder of William Dazley by his wife. One hopes these sentiments were not in the mind of the jury when they decided Sarah Dazley was guilty, for there is no evidence to prove women have a 'natural turn' to poison any more than men.

Murder is a wicked crime, murder by poisoning particularly so. There are rarely any witnesses, indeed stealth and secrecy are the main ingredients — along with poison, of course. A motive might be established, if it isn't already apparent.

Ah, yes: motive. In the analysis of a case, motive is always sought, and rightly so. Money, love, revenge. But motive may or may not form part of the evidence, supporting the fact that so-and-so committed the crime, and why. Motive is not an essential ingredient.

Evidence of fact is what counts. In the Dazley case, it came down not to motive — indeed, none was ever established — but the testimony of witnesses who, together, built up the case against her.

Caricature of the Execution of Sarah Dazley

15

2

Bedford Gaol 1660–1672

Persecuted for his Beliefs

The Story of John Bunyan

When at first I took my pen in hand
Thus for to write, I did not understand
That I at all should make a little book...
(John Bunyan: The Apology, The Pilgrim's Progress)

Crime may be defined as 'a violation of law; an act punishable by law'. Thus, in 17th-century England, in violating the law of the land at that time, *to wit* preaching in a location other than the approved, or 'established', Church of England, John Bunyan was a criminal, and as such he was punished. So were hundreds, and possibly thousands, of others, Dissenters as they were called. But whilst the 'injured party' in any crime is the individual against whom the crime is perpetrated, the state is also 'injured'. Yet, in the Dissenters' case, one wonders if the entire process was the wrong way around. A violation of law, yes. Justice, hardly.

Whatever he was and whatever he did, John Bunyan didn't seem to be a man who would harm anyone or steal anything. Nor was he a traitor to his country or a known pervert. But, yes, he broke the law; and, what's more, he could have hanged for his trouble. In fact, it's a wonder he didn't.

17

John Bunyan was a Bedfordshire man. He was born at Elstow in 1628, the son of a tinker. He learned to read and write, unusually then for one born into his class, and took his father's trade. When he was sixteen his mother died and he angrily left home when his father remarried. It seems he joined Cromwell's Parliamentary forces and was 'deeply moved' when a comrade standing in for him was shot dead.

He returned home the following year (1645) and married a local girl. She was poor, but she brought with her to the family household two books that had belonged to her father. These books and Bunyan's deep religious experiences may have been the time when the aspiring cleric and author set off on life's long road of preaching the gospel, and by the time he was 27 he could be found doing just that in the villages of Bedfordshire and elsewhere.

Events in 1646 would influence Bunyan's religious leanings when John Gifford, a major in the Royalist army, escaped from prison in Maidstone where he awaited execution. His crime: that he with eleven others had founded the Independent Church. Whilst not entering into the elaborate doctrines of religion, suffice to say that during the throes of 17th-century church reform, the Independents, among others, like the Quakers, advocated decentralised authority in the Church. So Gifford went to Bedford and 'obtained' St John's Church for his congregation, and in 1653, the 'tolerant year', and for some years after, it seems the authorities turned a blind eye to those involved with independent church movements, probably due to the Declaration of Indulgence by Charles II who made promises about religious 'tolerance'.

But Charles II was in no position to say or do anything that carried any real authority, as he had been in exile since 'inheriting' the throne upon the execution of his father, Charles I, in 1649. The monarchy had officially been abolished by Parliament, being declared 'unnecessary, burdensome and dangerous to the liberty, safety and interests of the people'. Charles II was abroad, wandering

Elstow Abbey

the countries of western Europe, the Stuart king-in-waiting.

Charles's Declaration – we should consider it, after all he was King of England – was that 'because the passions and uncharitableness of the times have produced several opinions on religion by which men are engaged in animosity against each other, we declare a liberty to tender consciences that no man shall be disquieted or called in question for differences of opinion in the matter of religion'. His Declaration screamed freedom to follow one's own religious leanings, and was reasonable, you might think. However, he added the reservation that: 'we shall be ready to consent to such an Act of Parliament, as upon mature deliberation shall be offered to us, for the full granting of that indulgence'.

In other words, he couldn't make it law just yet because he was barred from the throne and Parliament would have to sanction it first. But the promise to do so seemed to be there if ever he returned to England. It seems Bunyan and his ilk presupposed he would, and that the Declaration would then take effect. But let's look at the law of the time, notwithstanding Charles's apparent intentions.

In 1593, during the reign of Queen Elizabeth I, an Act was passed 'to retain Her Majesty's subjects in due obedience', making it unlawful to refuse to attend church for a month, and outlawing the attendance at assemblies and meetings under colour or pretence of any exercise of religion, stating that every person offending (i.e. not going to church) and being convicted, to be committed to prison and to remain there, without bail, until they conformed and attended a church or chapel or place of common prayer and hear divine service. Further, if within three months of conviction they had not attended divine service and made a public confession, they would be judged a felon. Maximum punishment: death. Land of the free didn't apply in those days: you went to the established church, i.e. the Church of England, or you went to jail.

It seems safe to say that aside from 1653 and for a few years at least, failure to attend the established church was a serious crime indeed.

Which was the problem with John Gifford's church in Bedford: it wasn't 'established'.

In 1653 Bunyan joined Gifford's congregation. In 1654 he and his family moved to a cottage in St Cuthbert's Lane, Bedford. Soon after, his wife died, leaving him to bring up four children. Gifford died the same year and was replaced by John Burton. The following year Burton started to spend an hour a week 'exhorting' prisoners in the County gaol, an act which another time might have led to him being incarcerated with them – for preaching outwith the established church, presumably. In 1658 the writing was on the wall when he was indicted for 'preaching' at Eaton Socon, although the charge was dropped.

In 1659 Bunyan married his second wife, Elizabeth. The following year, with Cromwell dead and his successors unable to find a suitable replacement, and after sterling work by General George Monck who favoured the restoration of the king, Charles II took his place on the throne. Great news, it seemed, for the Independent Church (and others), except that Parliament, which held real power, refused to sanction his Declaration of Indulgence. Charles wanted 'toleration', while the Church of England wanted to retain its powerful position as the one church, the only church. But why?

Charles II was a Stuart, which meant his religious sympathies lay with Roman Catholicism. This would be a direct threat to the Church of England's role if, shall we say, the Stuart dynasty secured a strong foothold in England's religious affairs. 'Tolerance' was not to be tolerated. The Independents and others – Quakers, for example – could not be permitted free rein.

So, in 1660, St John's Church, Bedford, was restored to the Church of England. That same year, John Burton, its pastor, died. Bunyan kept on preaching, and in November was arrested preaching at a farmhouse at Ampthill and thrown into prison. A man of God, yes. A criminal, yes, in the eyes of the law. A true criminal, hardly, for shouldn't all men be free? Bunyan was no longer free, but Francis

John Bunyan

Wingate, who committed him for trial, was prepared to grant bail if he would stop preaching. Bunyan refused, declaring: 'I should not leave speaking the word of God.' The following January he appeared at the Quarter Sessions before Justice Kelying, a man with a reputation as a bully and, like all bullies in a privileged position, was suitably placed to be his natural self.

The charge was 'That he (Bunyan) had devilishly and perniciously abstained from coming to church to hear divine service, and that he was a common upholder of unlawful meetings to the disturbance and distraction of the good subjects of this kingdom'. Bunyan admitted the facts but did not plead guilty. Kelying, attempting to clarify the situation, asked him if what he said was a confession. Bunyan said he only then realised he had been indicted. In the end the court declared it didn't know if he had pleaded guilty or not guilty, but regarded what he said as a confession. He was guilty then!

'Thou deservest to live no longer but to be slain immediately,' said Kelying. 'You must be had back to prison and there lie for three months following. If you submit to go to church to hear divine service, and leave your preaching, you must be banished from the realm. And if, after such a day as shall be appointed to you to be gone, you shall be found in this realm without special licence from the king, you must stretch by the neck for it.' A harsh punishment: to be thrown out of his native land if he complied and hanged if he returned – but the entire proceedings were a farce, since Kelying had no authority to pass the sentence. They sent Bunyan back to prison to serve three months anyway, with the option that any time he could agree to attend the recognised church. He refused. Just before he was due for release, Paul Cobb called at the prison to see him.

Cobb was Clerk of the Peace. He, too, tried to persuade Bunyan to conform, probably acting out of kindness rather than taking on the mantle of oppressor. To no avail, let it be said. Meanwhile, when Charles II was formally crowned king, Bunyan, and others like him, expected the 'Coronation Pardon'. No pardon came for Bunyan because he said he was not guilty of anything in the first place.

In the end Bunyan was unofficially paroled, that is to say he was freed by his jailer, who seemed to have some sympathy for him. Jailers must have wielded some power in those days. When word got out some of those in authority threatened the jailer with imprisonment. Bunyan, undeterred by the obvious risk of further incarceration, resumed his preaching. He hoped for a hearing at assizes but Paul Cobb removed his name from the court calendar, probably to avoid the case being heard and so prevent him being hanged.

Thereafter, for more than eleven years, John Bunyan was imprisoned for his preaching, saying that he was 'able to bear loss of liberty and the constant threat of death due to his conviction that he was God's instrument'. At one point it seemed likely that he would be freed absolutely, as indeed he was – for a time. In March, 1672, the king's Declaration of Indulgence belatedly became law, and Bunyan was free not only to go back to his family but to obtain a licence to preach. His congregation met in a barn next to St Cuthbert's Church, Bedford, on a site now occupied by the Bunyan Meeting.

Unfortunately, the Declaration was revoked after only a year, and licences were withdrawn. A warrant was drawn up for Bunyan's arrest, although it was probably never executed. Instead, the justices decided to leave Bunyan to the mercies of the Church, a far worse fate, it seems, than the courts could have meted out. Sure enough, the Church stepped in and he was once more incarcerated, this time in Bedford town gaol. Here it was he began to write 'The Pilgrim's Progress', his vision of life recounted allegorically as the narrative of a journey. In it, Bunyan's characters, or some of them, were those he had encountered in the legal system – with different names, of course.

In all the years he spent in prison, Bunyan worried about the plight of his second wife and his four children, the eldest of whom was blind. What his wife and family thought of a cause that took away the liberty of their breadwinner one can only imagine. Later, during

John Bunyan's statue, Bedford

a period of Bunyan's release, Charles II died, and Bunyan and his fellow Dissenters hoped his successor, James II, would approve greater religious freedom. Alas, this did not happen, and Bunyan, who would never give up his preaching, expected arrest and death. Instead, he was allowed freedom to preach, although whether by design, oversight or indifference is not clear. In August, 1688, aged 60, he died at a friend's house at Snow Hill, London. Whatever you make of the man, and his religious beliefs for that matter, he stuck by his principles. Principles that made him a criminal. As for 'The Pilgrim's Progress', it found its way into the homes of many, even the poor and illiterate. It can be said that Bunyan's work speaks volumes.

The Verdict

Freedom is something we may take for granted. We should not. Freedom is something John Bunyan did not have.

Freedom of speech, that is. Freedom to say what he liked, where he liked, when he liked. He chose to preach the gospel elsewhere than the established church, and so broke the law of the day. An unfair law, by any standard, laid down and enforced by unelected people – the so-called established church and an undemocratic parliament. They had no right to lock up those who sought no more than their basic rights. They, not hapless individuals, were guilty of crime. John Bunyan was guilty of nothing.

A Passionate Plea

It is commonplace for representatives of a convicted person to appeal to learned judges, either against sentence or conviction, or in some other matter on the their client's behalf. One's spouse would hardly be expected to make a plea, but perhaps in past times this was normal. As a prisoner, John Bunyan wrote about an exchange between his wife and the judges at the assizes in August, 1661, when she appeared before them to plead for his release.

Judge Twisdon told Bunyan's wife that her husband was a convicted prisoner and could not be released unless he would promise to preach no more. After more consultation, she appeared before two judges and a panel of justices. One can imagine her feelings as, with 'trembling heart', the poor woman addressed the all-powerful assembly of wigs and worthies.

Bunyan's wife: 'I make bold to come to your Lordships to know what may be done with my husband.' Lord Hales: 'Woman, I told thee I could do thee no good, because they have taken that for a conviction, which thy husband spoke of at the Sessions.'

'My Lord, he is kept unlawfully in prison. They never asked him whether he is guilty or no. Neither did he confess.' An unnamed justice: 'My Lord, he was lawfully convicted.' Wife: 'It is false, for when they said to him, "do you confess?" he said he had been a preacher at several meetings, and they had God's presence among them.' Judge Twisdon: 'Your husband is a breaker of the peace and is convicted by law.' Wife: 'It is false. A word of discourse they took for a conviction.' Judge Chester: 'Will your husband leave preaching? If he will do so, send for him.' Wife: 'He dares not leave preaching as long as he can speak.'

She said her husband desired to live peaceably, to follow his calling that his family might be maintained. She had four children (she was their stepmother), one blind, and had nothing to live on but charity. Judge Twisdon said she was making poverty her cloak, that he understood her to be better maintained by her husband's preaching than by his calling as a tinker. The judges advised her to have her husband sue for pardon. 'He preacheth nothing but the word of God,' she said. 'His doctrine is the doctrine of the devil,' replied Judge Twisdon, 'send her away.'

Later, Mrs Bunyan declared, 'I could not break forth into tears, not so much because they were so hard-hearted against me and my husband, but to think what a sad account such poor creatures will have to give at the coming of the Lord, when they shall answer for all things.' Alas, of that encounter there is no record.

3

DOMESTIC VIOLENCE (1)

Luton 1859–60

The Joseph Castle Case

Domestic violence. A modern term for an old problem. 'Domestics', as the police say about disputes between husband and wife, or two partners. Until quite recent times, police regarded domestics as a nuisance, and acted if only to try and restore the peace, or perhaps secure the safety of a wife. Nowadays, officers are better trained, or should be, for domestics can result in serious crime. Take the case of Joseph Castle and his wife, Jane. They quarrelled, she left home, he followed her and stabbed her to death near to what is now the perimeter of Luton Airport.

It was 19th-century England and this was a wicked crime. Premeditated, callous, then denied by Castle who attempted to persuade the jury that his wife had attacked him and then committed suicide. He was 24, a maltster by trade, and lived with his 21-year-old wife at his uncle's house at Ware, Hertfordshire. They had been married about two years. By all accounts he visited public houses, but did not drink excessively. Drink played no part in this crime (as it doesn't in most 'domestics'). But he had one weakness, that of jealousy. He constantly doubted his wife's fidelity. It was groundless paranoia, at least according to witnesses, including those of his own family. According to his aunt, Frances Castle, 'Jane never did anything except a little bit of sewing.' Gripped by baseless belief, he even tore his wife's clothes to prevent her going outdoors.

Just the same, tired of her husband's jealousy and their endless 'wrangling', Jane Castle left the house – and her husband – about 11 a.m. on the morning of 8th August, 1859, when her husband was at work and set off, on foot, to stay with her mother at Luton, 24 miles away. This was hardly surprising, since every bout of ill-treatment by him upon her was followed by making up afterwards, only to be followed by further 'brutality'. Enough was enough. How many will recognise these symptoms of a 'domestic'?

That she was afraid of her husband is borne out by the fact that she asked his uncle's daughter to accompany her, which the young woman did as far as Hertford. Alone, Jane reached Cromer Hyde, where, 'weary and distressed', she called on Mrs Archer, a schoolmistress, whom she knew. She rested there for two hours, then got a lift on a coal cart for a few miles, reaching her mother's house at Luton about nine o' clock that evening. Her father was in London, and that was a pity. Just the same, she must have been much relieved to reach sanctuary, where she slept the night through, only to find her husband in her bedroom at seven o'clock the following morning. He had come to fetch her and to kill her.

'You are surely not going with him. He will murder you,' said Jane's sister. 'He may as well murder me one way as the other,' said Jane. At 10.30 Joseph and Jane Castle left the house in York Street, although it seems doubtful that she intended to return to Ware with him, as she left her clothing at her mother's house. Maybe she agreed to walk part-way. They were seen walking past the Windmill public house by the landlord, who knew Castle. She was walking a few yards behind her husband, looking dejected. They crossed what is now Airport Way, and headed towards Someries Hill. On a farm road, just over the hill and out of sight of Luton, Jane Castle fought a desperate battle for her life. It was a battle she lost and her husband, having killed her, walked on to Welwyn where he gave himself into the

Someries Castle, near the scene of the crime

custody of Constable John Bennett who locked him up. Said Castle, 'If her throat is cut she has done it herself, but she has cut my hand.'

Reporting on the murder, arrest and inquest, the Bedfordshire Mercury described Castle as an 'inhuman monster', a presumption of guilt well in advance of his trial. Nevertheless, the coroner's jury returned a verdict of 'Wilful murder against Joseph Castle', and this was hardly surprising: the inquest was told that Jane had been grabbed on the farm road, where she had struggled and where she had been stabbed; she then ended up in a shallow dell where she was stabbed again and where her body was found, still warm. Her hands had been cut in a 'frightful manner', proof of her desperate attempts to stave off the thrusts of the knife.

The following March, Joseph Castle stood trial at the Shire Hall, Bedford. He pleaded not guilty. Despite facing the daunting prospect of a trial for his life, he seemed more concerned about the prospect of the crowd seeing him as he was taken from the jail to the court. To allay his worries, two prison officers disguised as 'gentlemen' stepped sprightly into a cab at the prison gate, along with Castle himself, also disguised. Outside the court they alighted in full view of the crowd and passed unnoticed into the Shire Hall. They were described as 'three swells from London'. Once in the dock, however, Castle was described as 'a very coarse, ordinary-looking person, with an expression of his countenance of thorough callousness, partaking very much of the animal and little of the human face divine. He did not betray the slightest emotion and like the fabled Vampire seemed to have fattened on the blood of his victim, for he appeared two stones heavier now than at the time he entered the prison'. Thankfully, the person who wrote those words was not serving on the jury.

The case was straightforward enough. Castle and his wife had left her parents' house in Luton, and a mile and a half away, in open country, she was slain. He'd given himself up, stating she had attacked him and had committed suicide.

Mary Ann Castle lived in the same household as Joseph Castle and his wife, at Ware. She was the young woman who accompanied Jane to Hertford. She said Jane had kept looking behind and was frightened. There was no denying Castle had set off in pursuit of his wife. He too called at Mrs Archer's, in Cromer Hyde, about 3½ hours after Jane. He enquired if Jane was 'with a butcher', presumably thinking she had run off with another man. Mrs Archer said she was not. Castle proceeded to Luton. He knew where Jane was bound.

Jane's mother, Francis Whitcroft, said her daughter's husband was jealous of a man she had never spoken to and she had been told that he had taken to sleeping with knives under his pillow. Jane told her the people she lodged with had advised her to leave. With this knowledge it seems tragic that on her daughter's arrival at her house she did not seek assistance, for surely Castle's imminent arrival could have been anticipated. In the event, Jane's mother went off to work at 6 a.m. the next morning.

Joseph Castle – Jealousy was his Weakness

Less than two hours after leaving her mother's house, Jane's body was discovered by two young women, who reported their gruesome find to a passing horserider, Thomas Stormer. Seeing the body, he did not dismount, but rode directly to Luton where he gave the information to Superintendent Pope who went to the scene. Dr Patrick Benson also attended. Their accounts of what they found are harrowing.

Supt Pope said Jane's body lay on its back, in the centre of the dell, with her head downwards, towards Luton. Both legs were turned completely underneath the body. Her throat had been cut, and there was an immense quantity of blood where she lay, and blood still flowed from the wounds. Her body was still warm. A bloodstained shawl and bonnet lay close by. He saw that there were marks of blood to a distance of 27 yards away, to a spot on the farm road where there had been a struggle so violent the surface had broken up. He found a small piece of bloodstained shawl nearby, which he was able to fit, jigsaw style, into the main garment.

Dr Benson described Jane's injuries. A wound extended from the left ear to the windpipe, so deep it exposed the muscles underneath. There was a deep-seated wound close to the windpipe extending inwards as far as the vertebrae of the neck, dividing the principal arteries, and this was the cause of death. He was able to insert his fingers. The windpipe was 'divided', a jagged wound as if more than one attempt had been made to cut through it. The body was taken to the Heron public house, where he made further examination, finding four or five superficial cuts on the skin. A thumb and some of the fingers had been cut, dividing tendons. A bloodstained knife, recovered 22 yards away in a nearby barley field, could have been the murder weapon.

He stated that in his opinion the position in which the body was found was as a result of force. The legs were bent back with the thighs resting on the heels and calves. She had been forced on to her knees and then backwards. The wound that killed her was inflicted where she was found. He was adamant the wounds could not have been self inflicted. Jane Castle was viciously attacked on the farm road, by someone wielding a knife. The knife belonged to James Castle, Joseph's uncle with whom they lodged at Ware. He readily identified it by a flaw in the handle, which he made himself.

On the road Jane had fought to defend herself before, probably, running for her life, reaching the shallow dell (an old gravel pit) where she was forced to her knees. There, her killer thrust the knife deep into her throat, so violently it reached the vertebrae. There was some opinion that she died on the road and her killer picked up her lifeless body and flung it into the dell. Whichever, the facts were hardly consistent with suicide: she causing injuries to herself on the road, then proceeding to the dell where the fatal thrust was made and then throwing the knife a distance of 22 yards before she died. Nor were the cuts to her fingers consistent with suicide. Jane Castle was killed by the hand of another. But was her killer her husband?

There can be no doubt that Joseph Castle was with his wife when she died, and that he played a part in her death. Apart from the evidence of witnesses and the recovered knife, there are the admissions of Castle himself that he was part of the proceedings. The jury was asked to consider three options: that Jane Castle committed suicide, that her husband murdered her or that he killed her in circumstances amounting to manslaughter.

Joseph Castle had told the police that his wife had tried to stab herself and that he had tried to prevent her from doing so. That is how he sustained slight injuries, he said. This unlikely account might, just might, have been believed, and Dr Benson at one point did concede that Jane 'must have been a maniac at the time', an allegation he withdrew (it must have been manna from heaven to the defence). Even if she was a maniac, she could not have killed herself in the circumstances that took place. The position of the body, the nature of the injuries and the position of the knife rendered this account worthless. Her husband killed her.

Castle also alleged that under 'influence and excitement', provocation if you like, he attacked her, perhaps in self defence, perhaps in anger. He thus killed her without express malice. But he stabbed her repeatedly over a distance of 27 yards. The jury was asked by the defence to consider this as the true account of how Jane was killed, in which case manslaughter would be the correct verdict. Then there was the likelihood that he murdered her. He followed her from his uncle's house in Ware all the way to Luton. The injuries to her hands were proof that she tried to fend off his attacks. She went into the dell where she was forced to the ground, those ghastly wounds were inflicted upon her neck and the knife was then thrown away.

The jury were sent out to consider their verdict. When they returned, after 15 minutes, a breathless silence prevailed throughout the packed court. 'Guilty,' said the foreman. Joseph Castle heard it dispassionately. The judge sent him downstairs, and when he came up again Castle was eating something. He was still chewing when the judge passed the inevitable sentence.

Once again there was a worry about the transportation of Castle through the streets of Bedford. It so happened that when the time came to move him back to the jail all the policemen on duty had gone. Before, the mob would have been curious to see the prisoner; now they would see fit to lynch him. Those in authority waited until the mob tired of waiting before Castle was moved without fuss from the main entrance of the Shire Hall back to jail to await his fate.

His fate, when it came, was that he was publicly hanged and his body was buried within the precincts of Bedford prison. It poured with rain but fifteen thousand turned out to witness events, a 'vast concourse who conducted themselves with decorum', at least until evening-time when fighting and disorder broke out. One man from Sandy was injured and was taken to the infirmary, and Mr Smith of the Angel Inn, in ejecting 'noisy country fellows' from the premises, was set upon and sustained a broken leg. Otherwise a good time was had by all, presumably.

The Verdict

Who could not say that Joseph Castle was guilty of killing his wife in the most ruthless and callous circumstances? To follow her, to take her from her place of sanctuary, to kill her the moment their presence was hidden from view and then say she had tried to kill herself. That's how he sustained injury to himself, he said; he became angry and killed her without intention. If anyone deserved to hang, you might think, it was Joseph Castle. But 'sound mind and discretion' is required before one person can murder another. Did his mind meet this requirement? Or was he insane?

The jury was told that 'no sudden burst of passion or mad jealousy would render a person irresponsible for his acts'. Was Joseph Castle incapable of knowing right from wrong? If he was insane, it was for the defence to prove it. They did not. There was no 'sudden burst of passion', not in circumstances that lasted over two days. Joseph Castle was guilty of murder.

The Execution of Joseph Castle

'He threw out his arms, clenched his fists and, looking onto the floor, his eyes staring wildly, his countenance convulsed with passion as if some horrible phantom had met his gaze, he exclaimed, "Wretch, wretch!" Then the chief warder asked him what he would have for breakfast'.

So reported the Bedford Times on Joseph Castle as he awaited his fate, blaming his late wife for his demise. He had left the dock as though he had been sentenced to a month's imprisonment. But later, with death looming, he was a man in torment. Was it out of fear of death? If so, he did not measure up to other, braver souls who, with all hope gone, awaited their fate with great equanimity. Or was guilt his tormentor, that he had said his wife had attacked him on the farm road that day, and that he had lied to save his skin?

On the day before his execution, Joseph Castle's mother and brother visited him for the last time. He was a murderer but she still felt a mother's love for her son. His brother urged him to confess, saying he would soon be dead and now was the time to speak the truth 'before he entered into the presence of God'. All three fell to their knees and the Chaplain prayed. Soon after, Jane's mother, Francis Whitcroft, visited him, begging to be assured that her daughter had not tried to take her own life, that she had died by his hand. He gave her the assurance she sought. Later, his written confession was made in the presence of the Chaplain. Its contents were never made public.

At 4.30 on the morning of execution, Castle woke and asked 'What time is it?' When told, he replied, 'Is it so late?' and then called out, 'Christ have mercy upon me, Lord have mercy upon me. Cleanse me from all my faults.' To his jailer: 'How many hours have I to live?' 'There are a few hours left to you yet,' he was told. Castle:

RIGHT **Copy of part of Prison Governor's Log on Joseph Castle**

"Castle" talks freely ab[ou]t his ordeal, &
also very [?] what he says, He
wished me to photograph him, which I
have done, Few men can have been
deeper steeped in vice and debauch[ery]
[tha]n this man, [Th]e last few days
had very much disfigured his
[fa]ce by actually pinching [th]e skin
[off it] – it was found desirable [to have]
[hi]s hands confined which was don[e]
[by] [th]e sanction of the Surgeon for
couple of hours, he [promising?] to le[t]
face alone,

"Castle" much [th]e same in conduct an[d]
manner, he continues to eat and sleep
[wel]l, his face so much improved h[e]
[i]s quite a different man,

Visited the outgrounds of [th]e
[asylu]m at 10/45 p.m all things
[sa]tisfactory,

'Jesus, take me. Bring me to thy flock.'

Some extracts from the journal, kept by the prison governor in the days leading up to the execution of Joseph Castle —

Thursday, 8th March (pre trial): 'Few men have been deeper steeped in vice and debauchery. He continues to eat and sleep well.'

Thursday, 15th March (post trial): 'He slept well, scarcely moved during the night. He eat (*sic*) his breakfast (eggs, a rasher of bacon, bread, tea). He regards himself as an injured man. He says the world has been a burden to him.'

Saturday, 31st March (day of execution, set for noon): 'At 11 o'clock the complexion of his character appeared to have undergone a complete change. He looked wild. At twenty to twelve he asked me, "What time is it?" I told him. He put his arms around me and said, "Mr Governor, you have done your duty to me." At ten to twelve I asked him if he would walk with me. He said yes, if I would accompany him. We walked with a firm step to the fatal beam. At twelve o'clock the bolt was drawn and Joseph Castle was no more.'

Toddington, 1882

The Drink and the Devil

'I am guilty of cutting my wife but I am not guilty of trying to murder her,' Walter White told the Woburn Magistrates. 'I had been drinking all Whitsun week and had the *delirium tremens* from nine o'clock on Saturday night till five next morning. I did it unconsciously and God is my witness.' Did a 24-year-old painter, living in Victorian Toddington, really know that *delirium tremens* is disorder of the brain produced by over-absorption of alcohol, often marked by hallucination? He must have known it was something like that, for he quoted it as his defence to a charge of attempting to murder his wife, Mary Ann.

White had never knowingly assaulted his wife before. They went to bed without any quarrel about nine on Sunday, 4th June, 1882, and at four in the morning Mary Ann awoke to find her throat had been cut with a razor. 'Murder!' she cried, leaping out of bed. 'Let me finish it,' said her husband. They struggled, she receiving further injuries to her hand and leg with the razor wielded by her husband, as well as broken bones. White then let her be and went downstairs while she began to climb through the upstairs window.

Several of the neighbours heard the fracas. William Holmes went outside where he saw Mary Ann at the window, crying 'Murder!' She asked him to catch her, but he begged her not to jump. Blood dropped onto the windowsill below and Holmes went into the Whites' house where Walter, seeing him enter, turned and went upstairs. Ann Marsden lived next door. She too heard a noise from the White household. She ran to the back door and shook it. Walter White ran downstairs and opened it. Mrs Marsden thought his wife was ill and ran upstairs to find her sitting at the window with her throat cut and bleeding. White appeared again and Mrs Marsden left.

The doctor was sent for and came at once.

George Whitbread saw Walter White on the street and wished him good morning. 'What do you think I have been doing this morning?' asked White. Whitbread didn't know. 'I have been trying to kill my wife.' 'Hold your tongue and don't talk like a fool,' Whitbread told him.

Dr William Goodman Hicks, a reluctant witness, said that when he arrived at the house he found Mrs White sitting in a chair, rolled up in a blanket, bleeding from the wound in her neck. She had also sustained wounds on an arm and another on her left leg, four and three-quarter inches long, so deep it went close to the bone. Her left knee was dislocated and the tenth and eleventh ribs on the left side were broken. Her left forefinger and right thumb were nearly cut off.

Sergeant Quenby arrested White shortly after five o'clock, by which time Mrs White's face was smothered in blood. In court White said he told the sergeant 'it was the drink and the devil'. Sgt Quenby recollected him saying nothing of the sort. Mrs White said her husband had been teetotal for six weeks but since Whitsun he had come home the worse for drink nearly every day. White blamed the drink fair and square for his conduct. He was committed for trial, and at the assizes he expressed 'deep contrition' and was sentenced to twelve months imprisonment. It is as well for him his wife did not die, for he would surely have hanged, a fact well known to him. In August he hanged himself. A verdict of temporary insanity was recorded.

4

LUTON'S DEGRADATION

The Destruction of Luton Town Hall 1919

We're a jolly lot of fellows, yes we are,

We're a jolly lot of fellows, yes we are.

For we come from Luton town

Where they burned the Town Hall down,

We're a jolly lot of fellows, yes we are.

'There's probably no city in the civilised world which is unacquainted with the terrible scenes of rioting and pillage which disfigured the name of Luton, and turned the town's Peace Celebrations into a bitter mockery'. Thus reported the Luton News and Bedfordshire Advertiser, following a riot the previous Saturday night when the town hall was set on fire and burned to the ground, a scene that would be 'indelibly imprinted on all Lutonians'. The newspaper added that the premises of innocent shopkeepers were smashed and looted, and that the police, special constabulary and fire brigade were subject to attack.

The Town Hall, built in 1847, had long been a focal point for the community, especially those involved in the straw hat industry: manufacturers, dealers and merchants. It was chosen, naturally enough, by the mayor and civic dignitaries, for a banquet when, along with the rest of the country on National Peace Day, Saturday, 19th July, 1919, victory celebrations would take place following the signing of the Treaty of Versailles, signifying the end of the Great War. The celebrations in Luton would include a procession comprising five bands and decorated floats. Fair enough, except that the banquet was for the dignitaries and their guests, whilst those who had suffered the greatest hardship throughout the war – war veterans, many injured and disabled, and widows and orphans – would be confined to the procession.

The Federation of Discharged Sailors and Soldiers, perceiving the injustice of this, instead opted for a celebration of their own, a mass rally, parade and thanksgiving in Wardown Park. They invited the Mayor and Corporation to attend. This was refused by the officials of the Corporation, who invited the ex-serviceman to join in the procession instead. Part of the reason for refusal was the cost, £1,500, considered too much by the Corporation. Also the occasion, originally scheduled for early August, had been brought forward, leaving little time for a celebration at Wardown to be organised properly. There were other reasons, too many to list; but, in short, the soldiers and civilians would march, and the mayor and dignitaries would have their banquet.

How insensitive! Up and down the country, 3 million men were being demobilised, men who had fought in a war which they were told, 'would be over by Christmas'. Thousands had died in muddy trenches, whilst those who returned home were maimed or shell-shocked after the fields of France and Belgium. And what was there now, in Britain? Unemployment and hardship and, for many, the dole. Those who had suffered most would not have been pleased when those who had stayed home could have their banquet, paid for (of course) out of the rates.

The Chief Constable, Charles Griffin, foreseeing the possibility of trouble, appealed to 'all serving and ex-servicemen to maintain decorous order as soldiers and gentlemen, remembering that the children are looking forward to a perfect and happy day'.

The procession, which included decorated cars, set off from

Luton Hoo. It was led by the Chief Constable on horseback, and other mounted police. The day was grey with light drizzle – typically English when there's a 'do' on. Discharged soldiers, Comrades of the Great War, a separate veterans' body who had earlier declined to take part, followed with their band, and after them other groups including the Special Constabulary: the procession arrived at the Town Hall at ten past two. It was met at the steps by Mayor Henry Impey who read out the proclamation he had received from the Lord Lieutenant on behalf of the King. The Mayor said he was gratified that the Comrades, by entering the procession, had shown they were good members of the community and had helped make the demonstration representative of the town's war and peace organisations.

There was, in the procession, an 'official car'. It had been provided privately by a number of 'ladies and gentlemen' at considerable expense to be met by the Council. To these and others at the 'posh end' of the procession, the Mayor read the proclamation again. Then the Mayor and other members of the Council went into the Town Hall to join their wives and children upstairs, bolting the door after them.

About twenty minutes later the door was rushed by some men and women, soldiers in uniform and other people in civilian clothes. About 80 entered the building and ran up to the first floor, terrifying the women and children who were there. They threw chairs through windows onto the street. They were looking for the Mayor, but failed to find him and his family and his guests. They tore down flags and decorations and electric light fittings. They broke the windows downstairs, which incited those gathered outside. Mounted police arrived and drove people back from the town hall steps. Comparative order was restored and once again the door was closed.

Some of the men then made speeches at the front of the Town Hall. 'Inflammatory', it was reported, but in a free society one would expect the right to speak, especially as many had been fighting, literally, for the right to do so. They spoke about pensions, unemployment and other grievances. They complained that having returned from the front many of their jobs had gone to women under new laws introduced by the fledgling Labour Party, and even to German prisoners of war. There had recently been a workers' revolution in Russia: why not here? They demanded the Mayor and Town Clerk come outside and speak, but with a crowd estimated at over 5,000 they declined. In such an intimidating atmosphere, who could blame them? After a short while there was a message saying that if the Mayor did not come out a crowd would go to his house. This they did, accompanied by the police, but they left without finding the Mayor and no damage was caused.

The President of the Discharged Sailors and Soldiers Federation then met with the Town Clerk and addressed the crowd, advising them to go to Wardown and join the celebrations there. But most remained in the town where they got drunk, and shortly after ten o'clock one or two windows were smashed by flying objects.

At 10.30 bricks and other missiles were hurled through the windows of the Town Hall. Then a fire was started in the Food Office. Two men bravely put it out, but it was restarted and extinguished again and again until it became so big the fire brigade were called. When they arrived the crowd prevented access to the blaze, and even cut the hoses and attacked the firemen. Flammable material was thrown into the room to help the blaze: pieces of broken window frames, doors and even petrol. They also tried to damage the fire engine, which had to be removed. National Peace Day was certainly turning into something else at Luton.

There was no choice but to forcibly disperse the crowd. The Chief Constable himself ordered the baton charge and the crowd was driven back. Several policemen were injured, struck by crowbars, bricks and stones. Firemen, too, were hurt as they maintained their efforts to fight the blaze, some being struck on the head with iron bars or missiles. Chief Officer Andrews said: 'The firemen were

Luton Town Hall – before the fire

rendered splendid assistance by a number of discharged and serving soldiers, but they were laid out one after the other.'

The Chief Constable said everything had been orderly during the procession, and at Wardown, which he also visited. Then he received a message about trouble at the Town Hall, and when he got there things were under way. He remained there all night, and pointed out that in all the speeches made at front of the Town Hall on pensions, etc, not one mentioned anything about the memorial service, and said the speeches were inflammatory. The speakers, he said, encouraged those present to rush the building and fetch out the Mayor and Town Clerk. There was 'complete animus' towards the Mayor.

There were forty officers to deal with the rioting, plus the forty specials who had formed part of the procession. Amidst a hail of flying stones the police charged the crowd, many suffering serious injury. In the end they were reduced to just three constables who had to be withdrawn. Meanwhile, the Town Hall was doomed as the fire blazed away, so the firemen turned their attention instead to saving nearby buildings now threatened by the flames, and turned their hoses in machine gun fashion on to the rioters, the only way of defending themselves. As police and firemen were being treated for injuries, the crowd dragged a piano from a nearby warehouse and sang 'Keep the home fires burning'. Just after midnight the clock tower collapsed, followed by the bell tower. At 3 a.m., troops arrived and the mob dispersed. Early on Sunday morning more troops came and took control of the centre of Luton.

More rioting followed on the Sunday and Monday evenings. The police surgeon (with assistance) attended to the injured 55 regular police officers and specials, as well as 15 firemen and 14 civilians. The total injury count was 84. Some of those arrested and later convicted of riot, damage and theft were otherwise respectable people: a schoolmaster, a council employee of 18 years' service, the local cinema operator who had been awarded the Military Medal. Several women were accused of stealing goods, sundry items from odd slippers, odd pairs of boots, scent, an umbrella.

The rioters came from a cross-section of the community. Three examples. A man called Long with 22 years' army service was seen at the front of the crowd when it charged the Town Hall. He was heard to shout, 'Break into the – Town Hall... Now is our chance... Smash the doors in.' He was very hostile and noisy, said PC O'Dell. Long said he was wounded twenty years before, in the army. PC Wood said Long was in several of the charges, and he heard him shout, 'We have a thousand more discharged soldiers coming along. They'll give you something to go on with.' Clearly a threat, yet it was true. Long was described as one of the ringleaders.

Another man called Barrett got on to the parapet by the side of the

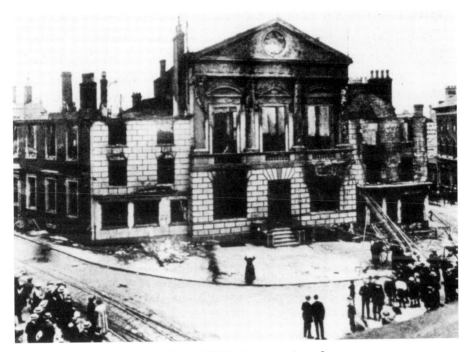

Luton Town Hall – the morning after

Town Hall steps and made a speech to the crowd on the Saturday afternoon. He had worked for the Corporation for twenty years. 'They had neither a soul to save nor a body to kick,' he said, adding that they were a lot of rotters. Sergeant Smith said he knew Barrett as a law-abiding citizen. He was 58 years old and had voluntarily offered his services to his country when he was 55. Sgt Smith thought Barrett was one who led the disturbances rather than followed.

Wilfred Harry Ovenell, 34 years, a schoolmaster, was seen in the crowd outside the Town Hall between the tram stop and the chemist's shop at the bottom of Wellington Street. There was a 'great mass of people' at that time, and the Town Hall was on fire. People were as close to the building as they could get without being scorched or getting wet from firemens' hoses. Ovenell was alleged to have thrown missiles at police and firemen. He was seen a few days later in a pub

Police at the burnt-out Town Hall

and asked 'if he was out to earn a V.C. on Saturday night or Sunday night'. Ovenell pretended not to understand. When Inspector Janes asked him if he threw missiles, Ovenell denied doing so, saying he had stood in the chemist's shop doorway to try and prevent people from entering. At the police station, he was immediately identified by a witness. He replied, 'I don't know whether I am guilty or not. I am all nerves through the war.'

The Discharged Sailors and Soldiers Association stated that they were 'in no way responsible for the lawlessness' and expressed sympathy for injured members of the police, special constabulary and fire brigade. The Comrades of the Great War said, 'Whilst not agreeing with the decision of the Town Council in refusing the use of Wardown Park to discharged servicemen, we deprecate the riotous and unlawful action of the mob'.

When the Town Council next met, it was announced that Mayor Impey had left Luton on the advice of Mr Smith, Town Clerk and the Chief Constable. 'Having regard to all the circumstances,' said Mr Smith, 'I am going to ask the Bench to send every man and every woman for trial and let them experience the weight of the law, and learn for once in their lifetime that there is a superior power to a crowd assembled in the street which is animated, as the evidence will prove, not by local grievances but by Bolshevism, anarchy, rebellion, criminality and drunkenness. If every person with a grievance was to do exactly as he pleased civilisation would go to the wall, and it would be impossible to live.'

Nor was that the end of it, said Mr Smith. 'On the Sunday night, at 9 o'clock, a crowd assembled in Dunstable Place outside the police station, and some of them had the impertinence to ask the Chief Constable whether he had a sailor in custody. They demanded his release, and when told there was no sailor in custody they were not satisfied and wanted to inspect the cells. Can you imagine anything more ludicrous?' They were warned to go away, he said, and because they did not, found to their surprise that instead of only a few injured policemen there was a large body of hearty men armed with batons who charged and drove them away.

Mr Smith said he could not conclude without stating his 'sense of bravery, personal courage, coolness and the intrepid manner in which our most capable Chief Constable dealt with the whole of the proceedings from the beginning to the end. Aided by his own men, by special constables drawn from all classes of the community, by the firemen, by such quiet and peaceable people as the manager of the public buildings, the Town Hall keeper and others. The police did all they could to obtain quiet without resorting to any troublesome methods until it was impossible to go on any longer, when force had to be exerted to repel force.'

Much was made of Mr Impey's departure from Luton, not least that he left for his own safety. Perhaps he did, but it was also probably to avoid any further disturbances that his presence might cause. He could not in any case have attended the meeting, as he was 'utterly incapable, owing to his state of health' after the riot and fire. 34 people would face charges, and the damage to the Town Hall amounted to around £60,000, although greater estimates were suggested. What was left of the building was demolished that August, and the site was cleared.

In all, 28 defendants appeared at the Bedford Assizes that October. The judge was Sir Frederick Arthur Greer. Nineteen were convicted and sent to prison, and two others were bound over to keep the peace. Judge Greer commended the Chief Constable on the admirable way in which he tackled this extremely difficult problem. He also commended his men and the fire service. A war memorial in Portland stone was unveiled on 10th December, 1922, in front of the space where the Town Hall had stood. In 1936, a new Town Hall, that which we see today, was opened on the same site as the old. Fireproof materials were included in the interior construction.

Luton Town Hall today

Stotfold 1830

Riot and Transportation

The introduction of threshing machines into agricultural England in the early 19th century was a Godsend for landowners. Sadly not so for their labourers, whose wages were low. After a harvest failure in the winter of 1829, workers were in a state of unrest and discontent. Trouble came, mainly in Kent and along the counties of the south coast. Hayricks and barns were burned, threshing machines were destroyed and poor law officials were attacked. By the time the trouble was over 19 people had been executed and over five hundred transported.

Bedfordshire seemed to have escaped this lawlessness. No threshing machines were broken in the county, although in October, 1830, some hayricks were set ablaze. But on Wednesday evening, 1st December, some labourers gathered in Stotfold, and after dragging reluctant folk from their beds and compelling them to join them the mob marched to the houses of the more 'respectable' inhabitants and demanded an increase in wages. After being told they would be seen the next morning they dispersed, but before daylight came they gathered again and went to every farm where they demanded that every worker join their cause and said no-one should work that day. Those not complying had their ploughs taken away, and one man who went to work elsewhere was cudgelled.

At 10 a.m. 300 men gathered in the churchyard at Stotfold. These were law abiding, working men, not just hotheads. They demanded payment of two shillings a day and when one farmer asked where the money would come from someone shouted, 'Damn their eyes, let's pitch into them!' Some farmers were struck, but they would not concede. A national newspaper, The Times, reported on the incident: 'The infuriated assembly proceeded to acts of violence and

53

demanded bread from the bakers, beer from the publicans and money from the inhabitants...' Houses and shops were forcibly entered. Even the vicar, who had recently increased his tithe, fell foul of their demands.

Things went quiet until that evening, when they went into the field – an open strip of ground – where they set fire to some straw. They declared that they would 'suffer death before any of them be taken'. They next day they went back to work. The principal inhabitants then met and W.H. Whitbread, a magistrate, undertook immediate measures. Over 100 special constables from nearby villages were sworn and dispatched to round up the ringleaders. Ten were caught and committed to the county gaol.

The trial was at Bedford the following March. Five men were charged with being 'unlawfully and tumultuously assembled at Stotfold, having conspired to obtain by force and violence an increase of wages...' The other five were charged with having 'feloniously broken into and entered the shop of Benjamin Howard and stolen a loaf of bread, value 6d...' In the days when the prosecution, not defendants, was legally represented, it may not be surprising that all were found guilty. Five of them were sentenced to death, although their sentences were commuted. Henry Gentle and William Sanderson were transported for fourteen years. They went to Australia on the good ship *Isabella*. It is on record that they found work straight away, married and had families. It seems doubtful that either man would have wished to return to England. Who could blame them?

RIGHT **A written account of the Riot at Stotfold**

Stotfold

On Thursday last one of the most daring desperate riots that have occurred of late took place in the village of Stotfold. Late on Wednesday eveng the labourers began to assemble together, and many of the more peaceable inhabitants were forcibly dragged from their beds, & compelled to join the rabble. They then proceeded to the residences of the most respectable inhabitants demanding an increase of wages, &c One of these gentlemen, however, had the precaution to tell them, that if they had any reasonable complaints to make they should be attended to at a vestry in the morning at ten o'Clock. With this understanding they seperated for the night, but long before daylight in the morning, they collected again, and proceeded to every farm house in the vilg; and compelled every man and boy that was willing to work to join them, and positively declaring, with the most horrid oaths and imprecations, that neither man nor horse shd proceed to work that day; which threat they literally carried into effect. In this state things remained until about ten o'Clock, when the Vestry assembled. They then demanded first, to be wholly exempt from the payment of taxes. This was agreed to. They next demanded the dismissal of the assistant Overseer. This was acceded. They then required that every man should receive two shillings per day for his work. This was objected to as a general principle; but as nothing short of recognising this principle wd satisfy the mob, the Vestry broke up after much fruitless discussion. The infuriated assembly (from 100 to 200 in number) then proceeded to acts of violence, and went thro' the village, demanding bread from the bakers, beer from the publicans, and money from the inhabitants generally; and such as had the hardihood to resist their demands, had a forcible entrance effected into their houses, and were eventually obliged to comply with their demands, or suffer their property to be forcibly taken away. Late in

The Verdict

The riots at Stotfold, in 1830, and Luton, in 1919, had one thing in common: those who rioted had, to some extent, reason for dissatisfaction: at Stotfold over workers' low pay and loss of employment through the introduction of new machinery, at Luton over pensions and other issues, aggravated by the conduct of those privileged council officials who would enjoy themselves at the expense of ratepayers. In each case it is not difficult to sympathise with the workers' plights.

The trouble with rioting is that, however 'justifiable', the focus of the rioters' cause becomes lost in the inevitable criminal conduct that ensues. At Stotfold, shopkeepers had their premises entered and their property stolen, and many of those who took part were forced to do so against their will. At Luton, councillors' wives and children, innocents all, were put in fear and might have perished in the blaze that destroyed the Town Hall, and owners of adjacent property, unconnected with workers' grievances, had their premises damaged and property stolen, whilst innocent members of the public as well as policemen and firemen, all doing their duty, were wilfully struck with iron bars and injured.

There are, and always will be, those who will take advantage of the temporary breakdown of law and order when a riot occurs, and never mind how 'justified' the cause. Rioting cannot be condoned, and those who riot must therefore be condemned. The rioters at Stotfold and Luton deserved to be punished.

5

LET THE PUNISHMENT FIT THE CRIME

I never saw a man who looked
With such a wistful eye
Upon that little tent of blue
Which prisoners call the sky.
And at every drifting cloud that went
With sails of silver by.
Oscar Wilde: 'The Ballad of Reading Gaol'

Punishment, it seems, is a time thing; the further back you go, the worse your fate. Whereas once upon a day punishment was harsh and usually excessive, today's criminals are punished comparatively lightly or not at all. Today, the weight of the law sometimes seems to be brought down heavier on the victim than the perpetrator. A criminal might even sue his intended victim. It'll be your fault when the burglar grazes his shin on the wheelbarrow you carelessly left in your garden. It wasn't always so. From being too extreme, we've gone too far the other way.

There was a time when you could be 'drawn, hanged and quartered', or burned at the stake. Gruesome, it is true. But there is no painless way to execute people. Consider:

Shooting. Evidently the most common, worldwide. Stand your murderer (or transgressor of whatever law applies in whatever country) against a wall or post and shoot him; or simply put a revolver to his head. It's straightforward and pretty quick.

Electrocution. A ghastly way to kill anyone. The prisoner is held with restraining straps, whilst thousands of volts are passed through the body. It's not a quick process, as the body jerks and may even catch fire. The prisoner may defecate or urinate or vomit, or do all three. Sometimes several charges of electricity of up to quarter of an hour are necessary to ensure death.

Gas. There are many cases where death is recorded as 'not instantaneous'. Lethal injection. Many people believe this is painless, but the veins of diabetics and drug users may be difficult to locate. If the prisoner struggles it makes things worse. It goes without saying that the guillotine was quick and, one supposes, painless. If you were going to execute someone, maybe the French got it right — or was it too barbaric? And, of course, there was hanging.

There are different ways to hang a person. Once, prisoners simply stood on a cart, had a rope placed around their neck and were left to dangle and choke to death as the cart was moved away. Then came the 'drop' method, where the prisoner stood on a trapdoor which, when opened, allowed him to fall and suffocate as the neck was broken, a relatively quick and efficient method, except there were times when the drop was too short and he died simply by choking; or too long, when his head might come off, as sometimes happened. Body-weight was all-important; hanging someone was a skilled occupation.

Execution in England was by hanging, or even disembowelling and 'quartering'. But even when things became more civilised you could hang for being in the company of gypsies, or even for being 'a child with strong evidence of malice'. In 1823 the number of crimes for which you could be executed was reduced to 100. Shoplifting was a capital offence until 1834. People would turn out in their thousands to see justice takes its course, much in the same way as they would a Cup Final today, many fuelled by alcohol, also just like today.

It was common enough to be hanged for theft, as John Jenkins was in 1683 when he stole money from John Wildes. Wildes said he was too old to fight and gave his purse to Jenkins, who took fourteen shillings then returned the purse, saying, 'God be with you and God bless you.' Being courteous did not save his life. Three people convicted of murder and hanged, all featuring in this book – Sarah Dazley, Joseph Castle and William Worsley – were commemorated by lace bobbins.

Thumb your way through the Bedford Gaol register, post 1801, and you will find that the poor are repeatedly the ones who fell foul of the law. And the poor then *were* poor, a million miles removed from those at the other end of the social spectrum, including those who meted out punishment. 'Let the punishment fit the crime'. But did it? A glance at the list of random cases taken from the Bedford Gaol register suggests it did not.

In seventeenth century England 'ordinary' crimes, apart from carrying the death penalty, would see an offender incarcerated. Then they found a way to keep the prison population down: transportation. A convicted person might be sentenced to death for the most trivial crime, enabling the authorities to transport them instead. No hanging, no occupation of prison space. The condemned would be sent to prison hulks, old sailing vessels moored in the Thames or at Portsmouth, to await the time they would set sail for America, and when the Americans won independence and understandably didn't welcome English criminals they were sent to Australia instead. Then came the day the Australians didn't want them either, and in 1857 or thereabouts transportation ceased. Out of 281 death sentences between 1801 and 1857 only 15 were carried out, most of those sentenced being transported. One can barely imagine the conditions aboard the hulks. Disease, such as cholera, was rife, hardly surprising when prisoners drank water from the open sewer that was the Thames.

From the 12th century the Church claimed that the clergy was exempt from the jurisdiction of ordinary courts, and that members of the clergy were triable only by ecclesiastical courts which could not impose the death penalty. Thus, if convicted of a capital offence (at the assizes) you could claim 'benefit of clergy', and could expect to be branded in the hand, a better fate than death. Proof that you were entitled to claim 'benefit' was simply that you could read. The usual test was to read the first verse of the 51st Psalm. Illiterate prisoners learnt it to avoid the noose. Incredibly, this practice was not abolished until 1822.

Over the years punishments changed. Some towns and villages had whipping posts (this practice ceased in the 1850s), whilst in Bedford prisoners would be whipped as they proceeded from the jail to the bridge and back. In 1668 a man called Thomas Hensman was whipped for stealing a watch from a house at Cardington. In 1675 John Gale was whipped for stealing a coat at Biddenham.

Stocks and pillories occupied our villages, as some still do although now for historical purposes only. Short, sharp, shock treatment, coupled with humiliation, might make someone think twice before offending again, you might think. Their use lasted until well into the 19th century. The stocks were for a prisoner's feet, the pillory for head and hands in a standing position. Then there were the lock-ups, or cages, where miscreants, often drunks, could be incarcerated for a limited period. Bedfordshire had its share of these. Silsoe and Clophill still have their lock-ups, in good order too. According to one resident, they could be used today as a deterrent to car crime. Quite so!

The practicability of the lock-up is shown in a case at Leighton Buzzard. It concerned one Thomas Thorne who called at the Cross Keys public house in the town 'for a row'. From the 'information' of Robert Pemberton, dealer in earthenware, 30th May, 1822: 'He was drunk, and called for beer which the landlord refused to let him have. He began to knock about the chairs and tables. Upon the landlady attempting to put him out of the house he violently assaulted her by striking her on the breast. A constable was called who took Thomas Thorne into custody'. And what did the constable do with the drunken Mr Thorne? He 'put him in the cage for making a riot'. In trying to escape, Thomas Thorne kicked the constable in the ribs.

One imagines the constable might have sorted that one out in the cage too.

A list of common crimes in 19th century England would not read the same as today: horse stealing, cattle and sheep stealing, highway robbery (highwaymen), poaching, housebreaking, witchcraft, rogues and vagabonds. Compared to today's drugs and paedophilia they might invoke feelings of the good old days, of times when highwaymen were gallant to the ladies

Village lock up, Silsoe

maybe. Don't you believe it.

On the 21st April, 1751, three men called at the Flying Horse, Clophill. They had horses and they stayed the night. They talked of

Ampthill Fair and purported to be horse traders. They spoke against highwaymen, saying they were afraid to move about for fear of being robbed or worse. The following morning they set off,

Key to Silsoe lock up – It is 6 inches long

Clophill lock up – Stray animals were impounded at the rear

CLOPHILL PARISH
LOCK - UP AND POUND

THE SMALL RECTANGULAR BUILDING
WAS THE LOCK-UP IN WHICH ANY WRONG-
DOERS WOULD BE IMPRISONED UNTIL THEY
COULD BE SENTENCED BY A JUSTICE OF
THE PEACE.
    THE ADJOINING BRICK ENCLOSURE WAS
THE POUND WHERE ANY ANIMALS FOUND
STRAYING IN THE PARISH WERE IMPOUNDED
AND THEIR OWNERS HAD TO PAY A FINE TO
GET THEM BACK.
    BOTH DATE FROM THE 19TH CENTURY

Cross Keys

Above the door of the former Cross Keys public house, Leighton Buzzard

probably for Ampthill, and went on to Houghton Conquest to a public house owned by a butcher. About 4 o'clock they left and took the road between Ampthill and Bedford and started robbing people on the road. One of them carried a blunderbuss and threatened travellers with it. They robbed four men of money and a watch. Then they robbed two farmers and a joiner on the Woburn road before calling at an alehouse at Maulden where they drank gin, and at the George at Silsoe where they drank three pints of wine — still on horseback — before riding off. When they got about three quarters of a mile up the road one of them was shot in the back, presumably by one of his companions, thought to be by the blunderbuss. He was dragged through a gate where he was finished off with a pistol shot through the head. At least one of the horses was stolen, a hanging offence. They were not caught. The good old days? Hardly.

Sutton 1808–30

Divine Right

Given the sentences handed out to the poor for what today would be minor crimes — execution, alternatively transportation; hard labour — one wonders about the fairness of the law, or lack of it, concerning Dr Edward Drax Free, rector at Sutton, 1808–1830. This man, born of privileged stock, was a fellow of St John's College, Oxford, and on taking up his post at Sutton embarked on conduct that at worst was criminal, at best scandalous.

Stealing lead off the roof the church, as he did, would have been more than sufficient to consign any of his parishioners to transportation or hard labour, but a member of the clergy could not

The Rectory, All Saints Church

All Saints Church, Sutton

be punished for such a thing. In his esteemed position he allowed sheep and pigs to occupy the churchyard, failed to preach proper sermons and cursed people in the street. He was a drunkard and a womaniser who seduced several housekeepers and made them pregnant.

One such was Maria Mackenzie, 28, appointed Dr Free's housekeeper in 1822. Soon she was sleeping with her master. She fell pregnant and miscarried. She complained that he knocked her down flagstones in the passageway in the rectory. He said she was pregnant when he hired her, and accused her of being a prostitute in London and that her miscarriage was due to venereal disease. When she demanded her wages he accused her of stealing a tablecloth and some linen and seized her property. Later, she looked up at the rectory window to see Dr Free had hired a new housekeeper, her sister! In 1823 he hired another, Mary Pierson. She left after nine days, complaining of his 'sexual overtures'.

One Saturday evening in 1820 the 3-year-old son of John and

Mary Saville died. On the Monday they sent word to Dr Free that they wished him to be buried on Tuesday. The woman with the message happened to pass on their request in the street, and was accused of being 'impertinent'. On the Monday the corpse began to smell, and on the Tuesday it burst from the coffin in the Savilles' home. Dr Free finally interred the child on the Wednesday.

When, eventually, the parishioners of Sutton were able to get rid of their rector, he refused to leave and barricaded himself in the rectory. They starved him out. He went to London, and in February, 1843, he happened to be walking along Gray's Inn Lane when the wheel of a chaise, driven by Mr Edward Rolls, came off. The horse bolted, and the chaise collided with a passing wagon. Dr Free was knocked down and taken to hospital. Nurse Lee, who attended him, said that over the next four hours, before he died of his injuries, he tried to speak to her, but she could not understand what he was saying. He seemed to be propositioning her, or threatening litigation perhaps, or maybe he was enquiring if there was an appeal to a higher authority. What a rogue! But for the privilege of his position, Dr Free would have been in Australia long since.

Porch doorway, All Saints Church Where the Rev. Free kept livestock!

6

LUTON 1867

"No more from your Unfortunate Brother"

Evidence of Accomplice

Street muggings, even resulting in the death of a victim, are so commonplace nowadays they rarely make the headlines. A sad reflection of our time, you might think. It wasn't always so. In 19th century England's dark streets, robbery of common folk was rare, not least because so many had so little to steal. It comes as no surprise, then, to discover a street mugging in Luton that resulted in the violent death of the victim was very big news indeed.

Not that we should ever be surprised when crime of any sort is committed by men who have access to watering holes in any town. The evil drink! One August night in 1867 at Round Green, Luton, William Bradberry was attacked as he made his way home, alone. And if this seems an uninteresting case, we would do well to reflect on the implications of the trial of William Worsley who was convicted and hanged for the crime, whilst an accomplice, Levi Welch, had the charge against him dropped and then gave evidence against Worsley, ensuring Worsley's demise. Justice itself stands trial here, and does not come out of it well.

William Bradberry lived at Lilley, just over the county boundary, in Hertfordshire. He was 48, a labourer. On the night of Saturday, 3rd August, he had been drinking in the Bell Inn, George Street,

The Royal Oak public house, Round Green
Drinking haunt of William Worsley, Levi Welch and James Day

Luton. He had been served four pints of beer, but most of it he had given to a companion who would testify that Bradberry was not drunk when he left the pub at 11.20 that night. Bradberry then went, on foot, to another public house, The Old English Gentleman, where he stayed briefly before setting off to walk home. He carried 'a bundle and a basket', he was on his own and minding his own business. By the time he reached Round Green there were lots of men about, and never mind the late hour. Most of them had been drinking too, and were making their way home. Included among these were William Worsley, Levi Welch and James Day, who were probably off for a night's poaching.

Worsley, Welch and Day had been drinking in the Royal Oak, at Round Green. The landlord, John Gazeley, and his wife, Mary Ann,

The Jolly Topers

were in the habit of ensuring the clock was quarter of an hour fast, and would say that the three left about five minutes to twelve, real time. They were not the only ones: several other men spilled out into the night too. But after a few minutes James Day returned, knocked on the door and asked for a lucifer — a light — as he had dropped sixpence and couldn't find it in the darkness. He returned again after another five minutes saying, 'Oh pray bring a light, for Worsley has kicked up against someone who is almost killed.' It was William Bradberry, who was dying of injuries to his head.

Those who saw by John Gazeley's lantern the injured body of William Bradberry would testify that William Worsley held him in his arms as he lay groaning and bleeding, and that he and Levi Welch lifted him and 'the blood ran freely from his mouth and ear'. Whoever had attacked Bradberry was probably present, or was an unseen passer-by who had fled. Bradberry was taken to the nearby Jolly Topers public house and placed by the front door, outside. Help arrived in the shape of Kitt Tomson, a surgeon, who came from his house. He had been told the victim had been 'knocked down, run over, some such thing'. He arrived at the Jolly Topers at 1.20 in the morning and had Bradberry taken inside. Bradberry was still breathing. He had a small wound in the centre of his forehead and a few abrasions. A few hours later he was dead.

The names of the men abroad that night are well documented. They had visited the public houses of their choice and were going home. Edward Gudgin, Daniel Kilby, Ben Scrivener, George Balls, George Layton, William Hucclesby to name a few. The latter would later say that William Worsely said, 'I found him when it was dark and kicked against his head,' meaning he fell over Bradberry. As any police officer would tell you, it isn't easy to work out what happened when someone has been attacked, especially on unlit streets, where people will be unlikely to see much, if anything. Men with drink will be confused, whilst the guilty party will lie.

No person was arrested that night. But there was a post mortem examination, by Mr Tomson, on 7th August. He found an injury to the back of the deceased's head, and when the scalp was removed he discovered an effusion of blood under the cut on the forehead. At the back of the head was another effusion of blood covering the bone and extending down to the neck and under the right ear. The muscles were 'livid' with the appearance of blackcurrant jelly. There was a fracture to the back of the head. There was blood covering the brain opposite to the side of the head where the fracture was. William Bradberry was killed by a smooth instrument, such as a gun barrel, he said. He was not knocked down by a passing cart, and his injuries could not have been caused by falling. Murder had been committed at Round Green that night.

Tomson said when he examined the road he found two pools of blood and marks consistent with the deceased having been dragged.

Evidence was given that Bradberry had left his house that night with about twenty-eight shillings in his possession, and that was now missing, as were the pockets of his trousers which had been cut off, and his bundle and basket. His body was identified by his cousin, Edith Cole.

Also testifying at the inquest was Worsley's sister-in-law, Mary Ann Worsley, who said that on the night of the attack Worsley came to her house twice, at nine and then eleven o'clock in the evening, and afterwards she noticed her garden winch was missing from a cupboard. Nor could she find it the next day. Earlier in the week Worsley had asked to borrow it but she had refused. The winch, which she used 'to screw the grate up', was a heavy piece of iron with a wooden handle.

The obvious motive was robbery. It was just a matter of who did it. The police had plenty of names to choose from and on 26th August, over three weeks after the crime, they arrested Worsley, Welch and Day. All three were poachers, and it transpired Bradberry was a part-time gamekeeper. It seemed possible he'd had a run-in with one or more of the group at some time. Also, Welch couldn't keep his mouth shut, and had evidently said something in public. They were charged with murder and sent for committal proceedings. All three denied complicity.

At Bedford Assizes the following March the charge against James Day was promptly withdrawn. He had not been with Worsley and Welch when the attack took place; he had been looking for his sixpence and there were plenty to support his story. A charge of robbery was added in respect of the others, who both pleaded not guilty to that and the murder. It was now that justice itself would effectively be put on trial. In short, the police had decided to focus on Worsley and drop the charge of murder against Welch. The jury was instructed to find him 'not guilty' and they dutifully complied. This meant Welch could testify against Worsley. Without the testimony of one there would be little chance of a conviction against either. The prosecution said both Worsley and Welch had robbed Bradberry, but killing him was down to Worsley alone. Welch would say so too, which is hardly surprising as by doing so ensured he could not be convicted of murder.

On 28th August the police, searching the area, had found a shirt, a piece of paper and some ribbon in the hedgerow, all belonging to Bradberry. Given that this was two days after the arrests and three weeks after the murder one wonders if one of the accused was co-operating, and if so, why? Was he promised a favour — like we might drop the charge? Anyway, nearby they also found a shirt, waistcoat and a pair of breeches. The piece of paper was linked to the sale of clothing to Bradberry by a Robert Beercroft, who also gave him the ribbon. Then someone found a purse, and two pieces of a pocket, which matched Bradberry's trousers. PC Marriner found a knife in a nearby meadow. It belonged to Welch, who had thrown it there.

Mary Ann Worsley — the accused's sister-in-law — said that on the Monday after the murder Worsley had visited her house again and the winch was back in her cupboard. Worsley would say he returned it a week later, so one of them was lying or mistaken. Later the police said that Worsley, in custody, had made statements saying, 'I did not murder him nor rob him. It was Welch that robbed him.' He said Welch had a knife, which he threw into the field, that Welch admitted cutting the pockets out. It was Welch who 'put some things into the hedge'. Worsley said Bradberry was already on the ground and that he tripped over him, that Welch had gone on before him and had been near Bradberry first, implying Welch had committed the crime.

Mr Metcalfe, representing Worsley: 'I want to see Welch's statement now.' The judge: 'The prosecution don't want Welch's statement read out.' Mr Metcalfe: 'But I do, my lord.' Surely this could not happen today: a judge resisting the production of evidence, supporting the prosecution case by doing so. Mr Metcalfe got his way. Welch admitted being with Worsley. In his statement he said, 'Worsley knocked him down with a thing with a handle on it, which is used for the purpose of closing up a range to make it larger or smaller. When he knocked him down he said "Come back". When I got back Worsley had his hand in Bradberry's pocket. He took out a parcel and gave it to me. I ran down the road with it and hid it...' Welch incriminated himself there, at least to robbery.

After Day dropped his sixpence, Welch said he and Worsley carried on walking when he saw a man. He walked on but saw Worsley strike the man. He struck him with the winch. Worsley gave him four shillings and sixpence of the man's money. Throughout Welch's testimony Worsley was reported to have glared at him with a look of indignation and contempt, clearly defining his view that they were in this together yet he, Worsley, alone now stood on trial for his life.

Have we not a case of one against the other? Whom do you believe? Welch, because Worsley had the winch? Worsley, because Welch struck Bradberry and he, Worsley, then stumbled over him? It transpired that Welch had a winch too, which he admitted under cross-examination. His was smaller, but he had not declared having possession of it and this could be the reason the prosecution did not want his statement read out to the jury. Day, who searched for his missing sixpence, was unable to say anything. Worsley denied all knowledge of the crime. Welch admitted his part in robbing Bradberry. The defence put up a sound, reasoned case, casting doubt that the case against Worsley was proved. They only had to cast doubt, no more. They concluded by saying that the only evidence to say Worsley struck the blow was that of Welch. Despite this the jury took just twenty minutes to condemn Worsley to the gallows.

'I never add to the sentence any observation of my own from which any inference, either favourable or unfavourable, may be drawn,' said the judge (as though this mattered), before putting on the black cap and passing the only sentence possible: 'That you be taken from hence to the prison whence you came, and that you be taken thence to a place of execution, there to hang by the neck until your body be dead; that then your body be cut down and buried within the precincts of the prison wherein you were last confined. And may the Lord have mercy upon your soul.' Cries of 'Amen' rang out from the gallery.

Guarded against an angry crowd by a police officer holding a cutlass (imagine that today), Worsley was taken away. A petition was drawn up and presented to the Home Secretary, asking for the sentence to be commuted 'on the grounds of the unpremeditated nature of the crime and the worthlessness of the evidence given by Welch'. It was pointed out that Welch was 'a man whose career for the last sixteen years has been one of violence and crime, and whose own confession was that he had robbed the deceased'.

Worsley was married, and he and his wife had brought up a little girl, now 12. This does not debar him from justice, but Welch didn't even face trial for the murder. Up went the scaffold, then the executioner, Calcraft, arrived. Worsley's appeal for his sentence to be commuted was refused. Then, on the night before his impending execution, he 'confessed his guilt'. 'I patted him (Bradberry) with my left hand on his shoulder, but he began kicking me. I said to myself "I won't stand this" and I pulled the winch out of my pocket and struck at him. I did not do it intentionally to rob him nor yet to murder him. I did it to stand in my own defence. I believe Welch had previously upset him or he would never have begun kicking me. Welch was close when I struck him. I was the worse for drink.'

In a long letter dictated to his friends, Worsley expressed repentance and said he was satisfied with the judge and his counsel, and thanked the prison staff sincerely. He added: 'I must now bid you all farewell, and pray that this may be a warning to all of you. I hope my wife will pray earnestly to the Almighty for guidance and strength during the remainder of her days. I pray for the merciful God to forgive me'. It ended, 'No more from your unfortunate brother'. Signed: William Worsley. He was hanged at Bedford on 31st March, 1868. Welch, who had at first pleaded not guilty to all charges, now pleaded guilty to robbery with violence. He got 14 years' penal servitude, the maximum. A worse fate, you might think, except he only served three months before being granted a fee pardon. Didn't he do well!

The Verdict

If we can assume Worsley's confession, made in the condemned cell, was true, then he was indeed guilty of murder or at least manslaughter. But what about Levi Welch — was he innocent?

If so, and the prosecution accepted that he was, then we must assume that a man of violent character left the Royal Oak public house with Worsley and within minutes, when Worsley was battering William Bradberry to death bar, knew nothing of what he was doing, or at least had no part of it. Either he stood back, or he was unaware of what was going on, never mind he robbed the victim of his money and clothing immediately after the attack.

A 'joint charge' of murder stares one in the face, surely. But that would not have been convenient, for if both men stood charged thus then any evidence by one against the other would be 'evidence of accomplice', which is always unsafe, each laying the blame upon the other. Better one was a witness — i.e. Welch. There were no other witnesses on that dark night, no-one who could say what either man did or did not do, not even the hapless Day who was scrabbling about on the ground for his sixpence. If there had been then Welch's testimony against Worsley would not have been required. The prosecution needed a conviction and Welch was their means of getting it. Worsley wielded the weapon, he was guilty. If there had been no robbery Welch would have walked free.

A Public Hanging

Hangings were once very much public occasions in this country. Crowds turned up to see felons, traitors, witches and others meet their end. People went for their own reasons: to witness justice take its course, to express their support or otherwise or simply enjoy a day out. Alehouses did a brisk trade when there was a hanging. So did thieves and pickpockets, and traders selling trinkets and souvenirs. By the 20th century hanging had become a private affair, where the guilty were hanged behind the closed doors of the prison, often to the solemn tolling of a bell, with a black flag run up afterwards to confirm the deed had been done.

But there was an 'in-between' time too. A public hanging, yes, but not exactly, for where the crowd would see the head and shoulders of the condemned man or woman, when the bolt was drawn he or she would drop from view behind a wall or a shroud, leaving only the trembling rope in view. No longer could they see the twitching, writhing death-throes of the condemned.

William Worsley was the last person to hang in Bedford gaol by this method. Before he was executed, the Private Executions Bill was in progress through Parliament that would, if passed, ensure no more public hangings of any sort. They could have permitted Worsley to be hanged privately, as the Bill would surely become law, but they did not. At ten minutes to eight Worsley was pinioned and taken from his cell to 'the drop' where he bowed to the crowd, who could see only his head and shoulders, and the white cap was placed over his head. He said something to Calcraft, to which his executioner replied simply, 'Pray on'. Then Worsley was gone from view. The conduct of the crowd, estimated at 4,000, was described as 'satisfactory'.

Lucy Lowe

7

Stagsden 1876

The Lucy Lowe Baby Case

On the evening of Monday, 20th March, 1876, William Robinson, a gamekeeper, was in a field near Stagsden when he shot a hawk which fell from the sky and landed in a nearby plantation. When he went off to search for and recover the dead bird he found instead a parcel wrapped in the 'black skirt of a woman's dress'.

The parcel lay among tall grass, off the beaten track and not far from a gap in the fence alongside the road. He nudged the parcel with his foot, and with the end of his gun he drew back the outer covering of skirt and saw a flannel dress. Then he noticed a small, white bag that covered the head and half of the body of a baby, and looking closer still he saw the child's face and hands. Not surprisingly, he went directly for the local constable, PC Tatman, who in turn reported the find to Sergeant Mardlin at Turvey who attended the scene, as did Dr George Swinson. The dead child, a little girl barely three weeks old, was removed to the tollgate house at Stagsden.

Events would show beyond doubt that the child's mother was Lucy Lowe, who would stand trial for the murder by asphyxiation of her daughter. Less clear was the question of whether the child had been murdered at all, or had instead died of convulsions and been abandoned in the wood by her mother. On this issue, and what the jury would decide after hearing testimony, would Lucy Lowe's fate be decided, for murder was a capital offence. If guilty, the only sentence was death.

Lucy Lowe was the sixth child of eleven to Henry and Susannah Riddy. She was born about 1840 at Stagsden. Her parents were married at Stagsden parish church, as was Lucy, in 1860, to Samuel Ellis. Sadly, the marriage lasted only four months when Samuel died. Lucy had a child by the marriage and she and her son went to live with her mother. In 1865, she was married again, to Ellis Lowe. They were also married at Stagsden parish church. There would be four children of this marriage (according to Lucy's father). But Ellis Lowe left Lucy who, unable to bring up the children, had them placed into the workhouse at Bedford, save one who died. She then went into service. The prosecution would make much of the fact that Lucy Lowe 'was accustomed to children and knew their treatment'.

In October, 1875, after a span of several years, Lucy was lodging with Mrs Priscilla Hull, at Greyfriars Walk, Bedford. She told Mrs Hull that her husband was dead and that her three children were in the workhouse (her first was living with grandparents). On 26th October she went into service as a cook at the home of the Reverend Joshua Kirkman, of Hampstead, London. She left on 3rd January. What she told the Rev Kirkman and his wife about her reason for leaving isn't known. What she didn't tell them was that she was pregnant.

She returned to Mrs Hull's house in Bedford. At first she kept silent about her pregnancy, but after a couple of days she told her landlady that she was 'in the family way'. In Victorian times this would have been utterly unacceptable to the Kirkmans, who would surely have discharged her when they found out. Mrs Hull allowed her to stay to have her baby, and on 26th February Lucy gave birth to a daughter. It seems the baby was never given a name, and throughout the trial was referred to by prosecution and defence, witnesses and even the mother as 'it'. A sad indictment of all concerned, you might think.

The midwife who delivered the baby was Elizabeth Richardson. About ten days after the birth she was back at Mrs Hull's house to attend the baby, having been called because both Lucy and Mrs Hull thought the child had been convulsed. Mrs Hull said the baby 'looked very black and was almost dead'. Lucy told her 'I have not done anything to it.' 'No more have I then,' replied Mrs Hull, who undressed the baby and gave her some castor oil. The baby recovered. Lucy had no bottle to feed her baby, but used a spoon to scoop warm food from a cup.

About 7th March Lucy told Mrs Hull she would leave as soon as she was able, to stay with her father at Stagsden. She also said that she would ask her mother's advice on whether to write to her married sister, who lived at Derby, to ask if she could take her daughter. On Tuesday, 14th March, Mrs Hull accompanied Lucy and the baby to the railway station at Bedford where Lucy booked a ticket for Turvey. At the station Mrs Hull asked Lucy if she had remembered to bring the baby's corn flour but cannot recall her reply, if any. The 'vessel' for heating the food 'did not go with her'. Lucy also left behind the baby's night gowns, 18 diapers, two little shirts and the bulk of the child's linen. Very odd, that a mother would do so. Did she think she would not require these things? She carried a bundle, which Mrs Hull thought must be clothes.

Under cross examination at the trial, Mrs Hull said that when they had left her house to go to the railway station the baby was wearing under-clothing, a body swather and a long night gown. Mrs Hull carried the baby, which was wrapped in two small shawls and a larger one. These were wrapped around her head 'leaving a little place for it to breathe'. Lucy wore a waterproof like a large cape without sleeves. She would say the baby's face was exposed to let it breathe.

Just over two weeks later, on 22nd March, Lucy returned to Mrs Hull's house. She did not have the baby with her. She said her sister in Derby had come on the Saturday and taken her to her house the next day. She said her father had come to Bedford station to see her sister off on the train, but she, Lucy, had not called on Mrs Hull as she wished to return to her father's. This was two days after the baby's body was discovered. She then returned to her former employment at the Kirkmans', in Hampstead. And it was to the Kirkmans', not long afterwards, that Sergeant Mardlin arrived to arrest Lucy Lowe on suspicion of murder. The arrest was far from straightforward.

When Sgt Mardlin, in 'private clothes', told Reverend Kirkman of the nature of his visit he was not believed. Nor would the reverend believe Lucy had been pregnant. He refused to admit the policeman into his house and called the police. The Metropolitan Police arrived and naturally supported their Bedfordshire colleague. The Rev Kirkman then demanded to see the officer's warrant. He had none, and didn't need one as he was arresting 'on suspicion'. When Sgt Mardlin took hold of Lucy's arm to arrest her, the reverend sprang to her defence again, stating 'she could never do such a thing'.

Testifying, Lucy's father, Henry Riddy, recalled his daughter coming to his house 'on a working day' that March. She came alone, bringing a bundle with her. Since the visit was unexpected and the first since the previous October it may be presumed it was the 14th, the day Lucy left Mrs Hull's. Lucy said she had come from Bedford, but said nothing about a baby to him. He testified that anyone coming to his house (at Stagsden) from Turvey (where Lucy would get off the train) would pass by the plantation at side-gate. He was unaware that Lucy had been pregnant. Sergeant Mardlin told the court of the clothing found on the baby's body, and the bag, which was 'just large enough to admit the infant'. The clothes were identified by Mrs Hull as having been seen with Lucy at her house.

There could be little doubt by now that the baby was Lucy Lowe's. But did she murder her child? There were no witnesses to the events that took place in that wood, so what other evidence could there be? As today, medical evidence was vital.

Dr George Swinson had visited the scene, seen the body in situ, had examined the baby. His testimony included much medical data, but the question was: did the baby convulse or was she suffocated? And if she did suffocate, was it by accident, wrapped tightly in that little bag?

The baby, he said, was well developed. He saw the clothing and bag removed. The baby was enveloped in a black wrapper, and beneath was a white ticking bag drawn over the greater part of the baby, from head downwards over two-thirds of the body. It fitted closely to the child. The bag looked like coarse towelling doubled over and sewn at the joining of two edges. The doctor said the bag would prevent the baby breathing and cause suffocation. The colour of the baby's blood (seen in the post mortem examination) was very black everywhere, indicating absence of oxygen and death by suffocation. Also, the position of the baby's hands, which had been clasped in death, indicated symptoms of asphyxiation. He conceded that convulsions might cause death over a time of quarter of an hour. How would he distinguish death by convulsions from death by asphyxia? 'I should expect to find the membranes of the brain more congested in convulsions than from asphyxia.'

The defence challenged the doctor's testimony. 'I ask you seriously,' counsel said to the jury, 'whether upon the opinion of any country practitioner, however respectable, you are prepared to say this woman is guilty of this terrible charge.' (One wonders why they didn't call medical advice of their own). 'There is no conclusive evidence to show whether the child's death was owing to a second convulsive fit or whether it was caused by suffocation at all. That is an end to that part of the case, for it is for the prosecution to make out the case for the satisfaction of the jury beyond all reasonable doubt. It is not necessary for the prisoner to prove her innocence.

'The whole case depends upon this: what was the cause of death? Was it a wilful act of murder or was it a convulsive fit, by act of God, or might it not have been accidental suffocation...?' He went on: 'If this woman, when she left Bedford that morning, had formed a deliberate decision that the child should not reach Stagsden alive, don't you think she would have resorted to some more barbarous way of putting the child to death? The bag is not fastened in any way. It is suggested that she deliberately put the child's head into the bag and left it there. You are asked to draw inference from the slight evidence, but if you feel that there are two sides of the question and that one view may present an appearance which admits of the innocence of the prisoner, then it is your duty to say the case is not made out against her. It is very far from being made out here with anything like the certainty one expects and is accustomed to in English courts. The inferences which have been drawn for the prosecution amount to little more than speculation.' The child had had at least one convulsive fit, he said, so why not another? Or maybe, on a cold day, the child was wrapped too tightly in shawls and suffocated, or maybe she had put it underneath her waterproof to protect it from the weather and maybe the mouth became covered accidentally...' The defence, it might be said, had a field day.

There was still plenty for the prosecution to ask the jury to consider. If the child did die by 'act of God', why would her mother attempt to conceal the truth? Why didn't she tell her parents she was pregnant? Why did she tell Mrs Hull the child had been taken to Derby by her sister? She told Mrs Hull that the baby would have 'a fresh quart of milk every day' at her sister's, a lie. Why didn't she take the child's night-clothes and linen to the railway station when she left Mrs Hull's? Lucy Lowe admitted that the child was hers and that she was with it at the time of death. She was unable to testify in her own defence as those accused of murder in those days could not do so. Instead, she made a written statement, which was read out to the court:

"On the 14th March when I left Turvey station the weather was very cold. I wrapped the child in three shawls and carried it along until I got to the Stagsden side-gate, when the child had another fit and died almost immediately. I was very frightened and left it where it was afterwards found."

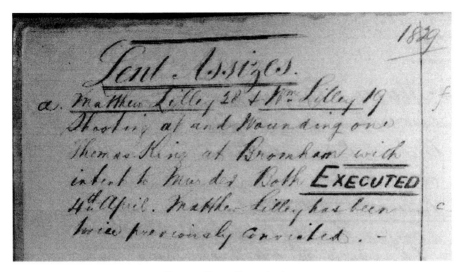

Extract from Lent Assizes

Facing the death penalty if convicted, it would be quite conceivable that she would be frightened if her baby died, and might abandon it. It was left for the judge to direct the jury. They had to be satisfied beyond all reasonable doubt, he said. The prisoner was not permitted to give evidence; it was up to the Crown to prove the case. There could be no manslaughter conviction: either Lucy Lowe had murdered her daughter or she had not. He stressed that the opinion of Dr Swinson was that the baby suffocated, and great weight must have been put on this. The jury took twelve minutes to return a verdict of 'Guilty of wilful murder with a recommendation to mercy'. Lucy Lowe, when asked, made no comment.

The judge donned the black cap, and 'in a voice solemn with emotion' told the prisoner: 'You have been convicted of the most serious crime, that of wilful murder, committed on your own child who should have received the protection and care and love of a mother. I am bound to say I am unable on the evidence to see how the jury could have come to any other verdict...' This latter opinion was his own and therefore irrelevant. He dealt with the recommendation for mercy by saying he would forward it to the proper quarter. Then he sentenced her to death. Lucy Lowe left the court without assistance.

The execution of Lucy Lowe was set for 24th July, at 8 a.m. But she was spared the noose, her sentence commuted to penal servitude, an escape from the gallows for 'a dreary experience of long life immurement'. She was transferred from Bedford to another prison. She may have died a prisoner. She may have been released after a lengthy sentence. She may have emigrated. Who knows?

The Verdict

D id Lucy Lowe murder her baby? It seems she probably did. If, as her defence counsel suggested, the baby died by a convulsion, then wouldn't she have sought help, or at least taken it to her parents instead of abandoning it in the middle of a wood? And why, when she took the train that morning, did she not take with her the baby's night-clothes and linen, especially as she was not returning to her lodgings? Surely a caring mother would have done. The doctor was certain about 'asphyxia' being the cause of death and if challenged, as he was, why didn't the defence produce a doctor of their own to rebut his conclusions. They would today.

B ut doesn't this case highlight the injustice of the old system whereby an accused could not testify in his or her own defence? Today, they have the right to do so, and this is the way it should be, for if they testify they can be questioned by the prosecution and if they do not — and they don't have to — then the judge must make comment about it. An innocent person would speak in defence, surely. Would you remain silent if you were falsely accused?

The Shefford Murderer

The Dilley and Rainbow Case

James Dilley lived in Shefford. He was a married man of 41. His lover, Mary Rainbow, was twelve years younger and worked in domestic service in Baldock. He had seduced her when she was 17 and she had borne a child. Now she was pregnant by him again. In 1879, the crime for which they were sentenced to hang was the callous murder of their three-week-old child, poisoned and thrown over a hedge, where it suffered a fractured skull.

Mary spent her confinement in London, in an apartment rented by Dilley. On Sunday, 11th May, three weeks after the birth, Dilley travelled to London and took mother and child from their lodgings. He told the landlady he was taking them home. Next morning the child was found dead in a brick-field in Hornsey, thrown away as one would throw away garbage. The gender of the child is not recorded.

Dilley and Rainbow were seen at Finsbury Park railway station, on the night they left their lodgings. They appear to have made their way to their separate homes, she discarding items of the child's clothing on the way. The clothes were recovered and used to prove the identity of the child. This must have also proved that Mary Rainbow knew of her baby's death. Whether she played any part in it is unclear.

Dilley and Rainbow were both convicted of murder at the Central Criminal Court, London, and sentenced to hang. The jury made a recommendation for mercy for Mary Rainbow, and 700 people signed a petition seeking her sentence to be commuted. Her solicitor maintained that when they were caught Dilley tried to throw all the blame onto her, that she might not have been in Hornsey at all and, if so, could not therefore involved in the murder. She pointed out that Rainbow would 'never betray' Dilley, but loyalty can be no defence to crime. She added that hanging Rainbow was 'inconsistent with the march of civilisation and the sentiments of humanity and justice', and that there is 'a difference between the destruction of a child three weeks old and the murder, in cold blood, of a grown up human being'.

What one might make of the last two points as an argument against punishing someone for the murder of a baby must be subjective. 'Inconsistent with the march of civilisation', perhaps; a 'difference' — presumably she meant it is less of a crime to kill a child than an adult, as she was seeking to have Rainbow spared — is risible. In the event, Rainbow's sentence was commuted. She maintained that Dilley took her and the baby to Finsbury Park station, and left her there whilst he took the baby away and presumably got rid of it. Yet, later, she was seen throwing its clothes away. Was she guilty of murder? We shall never know. She was spared the noose, but Dilley wasn't. He was hanged at Newgate on 25th August, 1879. He admitted the justice of the sentence and stated that he was 'glad his accomplice had been spared'.

8

*"A place of terror to those without,
of punishment to those within"*

John Howard and Prison Reform

'Prison is too good for them.' So people say of those convicted of many crimes, especially against children or the elderly, say. Given some of the horrific crimes committed, they may be right. What they mean, of course, is that in prison 'they' have television and (these days) mobile phones, when instead they should have, well, none of these things. Maybe those who say so are right. But have they ever stopped to think that those in prison have lost life's most precious commodity: freedom, albeit deservedly? What more should anyone lose, even criminals?

Locked up. Behind high walls. Sleeping in a cell. Slopping out. Prison is a punishment, yes; it is also a rehabilitation process, or is meant to be. One thing prison does guarantee is that when someone is inside he or she cannot be committing crime outside. So prison is justified. But whereas today they have it 'soft', it wasn't always so. Once, conditions inside were so bad, so cruel, that one might argue that those who sent people to prison were themselves guilty of crime: inhumanity. Prison conditions in 1780 England bore little resemblance to those, say, eighty years later when things improved. In this relatively short period prison reform throughout England made great steps, thanks mainly to John Howard, High Sheriff of Bedfordshire.

Howard was born in Hackney in September, 1726, the son of a wealthy businessman. His mother died when he was five, his father when he was just sixteen. The latter event terminated his apprenticeship as a greengrocer, after which he travelled in France and Italy. These were not the best times to be abroad in Europe, and in 1756 the packet ship on which Howard sailed was captured by a French privateer, and he was taken prisoner and cast into a dungeon. He had first hand experience of prison life, in France, before he was released. He married in 1758, after which he suffered tragedy when his wife died soon after the birth of their first child.

Howard was a Nonconformist. He lived at Cardington, near Elstow, where, perhaps not surprisingly, he was a member of the Bunyan Meeting for a time. As landholder, he provided good quality housing on the Cardington estate, ensuring workers had better conditions than elsewhere; also, he paid for the education of their children, not normally afforded to children in the early years of the Industrial Revolution. He became High Sheriff of Bedfordshire in February, 1773, a grand-sounding position but one with little responsibility. When he attended the Lent Assizes of that year, he was appalled to find that some of the prisoners who were acquitted were kept in jail. The reason, he was told, was that jailers had to rely for payment through fees paid by their prisoners. If they couldn't pay – which usually they couldn't – they stayed where they were. This appalled Howard, who must have reasonably asked, 'Why should an innocent person be kept locked up?'

He went to see for himself, and at Bedford prison he found a paper stating: 'All persons that come to this place by warrant must pay before discharge fifteen shillings and four pence to the jailer and two shillings to the turnkey'. As the majority of prisoners had no money, it was hardly surprising they could not pay. This unfair system applied up and down the country. Prisons everywhere were ghastly, smelly places, with no authority and no discipline. There was disease, hunger, poor sanitation. Howard described a jail thus: 'There is a day room for debtors which may be used as a chapel. For felons there are two day rooms without fireplaces, one for men, the other for women. Two dungeons down eleven steps, very damp. The straw for which the county allows the jailer £5 per year is not on the floors but on frames or bedsteads. On application the justices allow winter coals to felons and debtors'.

A 'Jailer's Bill' in 1731:

For beer at the Coroner's inquest	7 shillings and 6 pence
Paid the cryer fees	1 shilling
Paid a man who helped bring (prisoner) downstairs	6 pence
Paid two men to help lay the prisoner out in a coffin	2 shillings
Paid four men to carry him to church	4 shillings
Beer for the bearers	2 shillings

It cost more for beer than men's wages!

Howard recommended that jailers should be paid a salary from the rates, rather than by their prisoners. The magistrates were reluctant to agree, saying that the system at Bedford was universal and that there was no precedent for such extravagance with ratepayers' money. All Howard ever wanted were prisons that were well-managed and clean, with jailers and other staff paid from the rates. He did not endeavour to enquire anything of the prisoners themselves. In 1773 magistrates were allowed to appoint chaplains and pay them, and the following year they were empowered to select surgeons to attend to sick prisoners.

Howard spent three years collecting information, and in 1774 he presented his findings to the House of Commons. As a result, Parliament passed the Gaol Act, which abolished jailers' fees and suggested ways of improving prison sanitary conditions and prisoners' health. Despite this, magistrates were reluctant to implement these measures.

The Penitentiary Act, 1779, provided for, among other things, prison officials to be paid a salary, prisoners to be paid a share of earnings and be granted remission for good conduct. It also ruled that prisoners should wear uniforms, be subject to a coarse diet and that the work should be arduous and servile. Plans to build new prisons, including separate ones for men and women, were held up due to the cost of the continuing wars between England and France. Nevertheless 45 prisons were rebuilt pre-1790, although they remained under local control. Another Gaol Act, of 1823, imposed prison uniformity throughout the country.

Howard visited prisons in many European countries, finding them as bad as those in England, except for one, in Ghent, where conditions were far better and which he used as an example of what English prisons should be like. He wrote 'The State of the Prisons in England and Wales' (1777), which included accounts of foreign prisons. In 1787, John Wesley, the evangelist, wrote in his diary, 'I think Mr Howard one of the greatest men in Europe'. In 1789 Howard set off yet again, visiting more prisons. He contracted typhus and died on 20th January, 1790 at Kherson, in the Ukraine, aged 64.

In 1797, somewhat belatedly, Bedford prison was described as 'insufficient' and a new prison was built. It opened in 1801. But prison reform was not without its critics, who claimed that prison no longer acted as a sufficient deterrent to criminals. A debate raged: was too much being done *to* the convict, or *for* the convict? 'Prison should be a place of sorrow and wailing, and a return should be contemplated with horror'. Prisoners were receiving benefits denied to law-abiding families. 'Carpenters in one shop, tailors in another, weavers in a third, all sitting down to a meal... receiving a regular

RIGHT **Howard's statue, Bedford**

Bedford Prison

Today's county jail at Bedford was opened in 1801. It was built on land sold for ten shillings by the Duke of Bedford, and cost about £6,500. The prison held debtors as well as felons. It was built in the form of a cross and was too small, housing only 40 prisoners on the likely assumption that transportation of felons to the colonies (instead of holding them in jail) would ensure the population would not grow high. Executions had hitherto taken place at Gallows Corner, Biddenham; now they would take place at the new jail, although still in view of the public until 1868. It has housed the famous and infamous: James Hanratty was the last to hang at Bedford, and some of the Great Train Robbers were guests of the governor.

Bedford Prison today

portion of their earnings... it is better than life on the other side of the wall'. In those days, it could be argued that prison did indeed provide better security than outside prison walls. But prisoners were locked up. Was loss of freedom not punishment enough?

Although John Howard died over 200 years ago his legacy lives on. In 1866 the Howard Association was formed to continue to campaign for prison reform. Its aim was 'the promotion of the most efficient means of penal treatment and crime prevention, and to promote reformatory and radically preventive treatment of offenders'. In 1921 the Association merged with the Penal Reform League to form today's Howard League for Penal Reform. Over the years it has campaigned for, among other things, juvenile courts, the abolition of corporal punishment (abolished in 1948), improved procedures on suicide prevention in prison and the prevention of pregnant women prisoners being shackled (practised until the 1990s).

There are at least two statues of John Howard. One, which he had forbidden during his lifetime, stands in St Paul's Cathedral, London; the other is in Bedford, in front of St Paul's Church. It was erected in 1890. He was buried in Russia. On his tombstone is inscribed: 'Whosoever thou art, thou standest at the grave of thy friend'. A fitting epitaph.

The Firs, Leighton Buzzard (now Firs Path)

9

Domestic Violence (2)

Leighton Buzzard 1937

With Malice Aforethought

At seven o'clock on Monday, 12th April, 1937, Frank Cox, a railway worker, was walking from his home in Clarence Road, Leighton Buzzard, to Old Linslade, where he worked. His route was by way of The Firs (now Firs Path), which runs from Plantation Road. The path was a lovers' lane (and may still be), a convenient cut-through for pedestrians like Mr Cox. It was a fine day, so he would have expected a pleasant walk before starting work. In the event, what he discovered twenty or so yards along the path was not pleasant at all.

Lying at the side of the path was the body of a young woman. She lay spreadeagled, with her feet towards the road. There had been signs of a struggle and some of her clothing had been torn from her. Her silk stockings were pulled down to her ankles and some of her clothing lay at her side. Her shoes lay nearby and she was wearing gloves. It was apparent that she had been attacked, and that she was dead. Mr Cox covered the woman's body with his coat, ran to a nearby house and called the police.

When police attended the scene they found marks of violence on the woman's head and neck. There was slight dislocation of her nose. A black silk scarf with white spots was tied around her neck in a 'granny' knot, so tightly that when Dr Taylor, Home Office pathologist, tried to undo it he could not do so, and he had difficulty inserting scissors between the scarf and her neck so as to cut it free. There were scratches on the deceased's neck, consistent with marks made by fingernails when tying the knot in the scarf. Shock and asphyxiation were the cause of death, and there was no doubt that the woman had been murdered after a struggle on the path where she lay. Death would have occurred about three minutes after the knot in the scarf was tied.

Local police took charge of the investigation, joined soon after by detectives from Scotland Yard, led by Chief Inspector Barker. When he examined the scene he found two impressions in the sandy soil, between the woman's legs, as though made by someone kneeling.

At the inquest, which was opened on the Thursday, the court was told that the dead woman was Miss Ruby Anne Keen, aged 23, of Plantation Road, Leighton Buzzard. She lived with her widowed mother and older sister, and was last seen by her family at 7.15 p.m. on the evening before she was murdered when she had left the house to go out. She was described as an attractive blonde, with cropped hair. She liked dancing, and was a keen cyclist, sometimes going off on long rides with a friend. In short, she was a young woman in her prime. She was due to be married that August to a local policeman. Alas, for her, such dreams came to a sudden and violent end just yards from her home.

It didn't take the police long to identify a suspect, the man who was indeed her killer. He was Leslie George Stone, 24, of Heath and Reach, an ex-soldier and former boyfriend of Ruby.

Stone had lived all his life in the Leighton Buzzard area. He joined the army in 1930, serving in the Royal Artillery. Soon afterwards he met Ruby. In 1932 he was posted abroad, to Hong Kong, and although they corresponded for a couple of years she ceased to write to him. After service in Malta he returned to Heath and Reach in 1936 and was discharged from the army in January, 1937. On 28th March, when he saw Ruby for the first time since his

Plantation Road

return to England, she was with a man, probably her boyfriend. Stone did not speak to her on that occasion, but then, it seems, he embarked upon a course of events very much with Ruby in mind.

First, he ordered a new suit, and said it must be delivered speedily. Then on Sunday, 4th April, he met Ruby on the High Street and invited her out for a drink at the Golden Bell public house in Church Square. According to his testimony, she was pleased to see him and they enjoyed their drink that night. A witness, who was nearby, heard Stone say to Ruby, 'I will see you next weekend,' and she replied, 'All right.' The following Saturday he collected his new suit, and on the Sunday he was wearing it when he caught the bus from Heath and Reach to Leighton Buzzard. He also wore a light brown overcoat, but no hat, and was described as looking very smart. He was off to see Ruby.

It was just after eight o'clock when Ruby entered the Golden Bell, where she met up with Stone. Soon she would be dead by his hand, victim of a murder for which the motive seems obvious yet was never truly established. At first he would deny responsibility, then at the eleventh hour he would change his mind when he saw that he could not escape justice, hoping for a conviction of manslaughter, so avoiding the noose.

Word soon spread about Ruby's murder. Leslie Stone knew that he and Ruby had been seen in the Golden Bell and another public house, the evening before she died. He knew he would be an obvious suspect. So he decided to go to the police before they came to him. On that Monday afternoon, he called at the home of Constable McCarthy at Heath and Reach. The officer wasn't in, but his wife was.

Stone was 'very worried and agitated', so much so she gave him some brandy. He wanted to 'make a statement to clear himself', he said, and could she telephone the police station at Leighton Buzzard. He told her he and Ruby had been together the night before, but at 10.15 they had parted and gone to their separate homes. He said the same to the constable who arrived, and opted to make a written statement. In it he said, 'Between 8 and 9 p.m. I was in the Golden Bell when Miss Ruby Keen walked in. I bought her a glass of port. About 9 o'clock we came out and called at the Cross Keys, in the Market Square (now Lloyds TSB) where we had two more glasses of port. I left her at The Stag about 10.15 p.m.' That was his story, the one he had decided to tell. And he had come forward to tell it, rather than be sought out to do so.

The police needed to do two important things: to check out Stone's story about the movements of him and Ruby on the Sunday evening, and to examine his clothing. They did both.

That Stone and Ruby were together that night is beyond doubt. Lots of people saw them. They met in the Golden Bell and went on

Ruby Anne Keen

Lloyds TSB, Leighton Buzzard – once the Cross Keys public house

to the Cross Keys, which they left about ten (closing time then). It's where they went and what they did afterwards the police had to establish. Stone said that when they left the Cross Keys they walked as far as The Stag together where they parted about 10.15. He said she walked up Plantation Road, he walked up Heath Road to catch the bus home. He was adamant: they parted at The Stag.

On the jacket of Stone's new suit was found a piece of silk thread. It contained 38 to 40 filaments from Ruby's dress. The same material, the same colours. But this merely confirmed that they had been together – recently, though, for on his admission it was the first time he had worn the suit, on the Sunday evening. On the trousers were found white bristles, matching those found on a clothes brush in his bedroom. Both knees were impregnated by sand, similar to the sandy soil at the scene of the crime where someone had been kneeling. The left knee had lost its 'nap', apparently through being vigorously brushed when still damp.

It seems that the police could prove they were together, at least until shortly after ten o'clock. But what about after ten o'clock? Could police prove they were together then? Or, just as important, could Stone prove they were not? There were witnesses galore. Mrs Andrews, a neighbour of the Keens, said she saw Ruby with a young man with no hat walking past Ruby's house in Plantation Road (in the direction of The Firs). Miss Masters said she saw Ruby and Stone walking towards The Firs. She knew them both, yet failed to pick out Stone at an identification parade. She said she was 'too frightened'. Thomas Wilson said he and his wife encountered Stone and a young woman whom they did not know about 40 yards from The Firs. Other witnesses were in the vicinity of Stone's home at the relevant time and did not see Stone on the road, as he would have been if his story were true.

Stone was with Ruby on the night, they walked off together, the trousers of a brand new suit had been vigorously brushed at the knees, someone had knelt between Ruby's legs at the scene. Despite being far from watertight, the evidence against Stone, much of it circumstantial, was heavy. Stone must have thought so, for at his trial at the Old Bailey he exercised his right to testify, and when he did his defence counsel asked him, 'In the statement you made to the police did you tell the whole truth?' 'No sir,' he replied. 'You are sworn to tell the whole truth today. Are you prepared to do so?' 'Yes,' replied Stone, no doubt on the advice of his own counsel, and for a very good reason, if the truth amounted to something which would see him convicted of manslaughter and not murder.

He said that in the Golden Bell he drank three pints of mild, then in the Cross Keys he drank two more pints. Ruby had a total of three glasses of port. He admitted after leaving the Cross Keys, he and Ruby walked along Plantation Road to The Firs. It was here, he said, that they kissed, but then Ruby annoyed him with her 'little trick'. She used to put her little finger into his ear, he said. This annoyed him. She had done it five years before, when he had taken a swing at her, missed and injured his hand against the wall.

In The Firs that fateful night they spoke of her 'little trick' and him hitting the wall that time. On the night of her murder, he said she called him a dirty devil and struck him on the side of the head below the left ear. A full right swing with her gauntlet glove. Then she struck him with her other hand. 'So I caught hold of her scarf and I think I pulled it.' He added, 'I think I knotted it again after that.' The judge intervened: 'Was she standing up at this time?' 'Yes, she started to fall down and I caught hold of the front of her clothes.' His case of self defence was under way. 'I was in a kind of rage.' 'What happened to her clothes when you caught hold of her?' he was asked. 'They all tore off as she was falling.' He denied stripping her, but how were her stockings down to her ankles? He could not explain it.

He said he knelt down because he thought he had just stunned her. He then got up and brushed the knees of his trousers. 'Did you think she was dead or badly injured?' 'No sir.' The judge: 'Did you do this to revenge the blow on the face?' 'I hit her back.' Stone said he believed she was unconscious when he walked away. He went home and said nothing to his mother. The following morning, when he heard Ruby was dead, he went to the police of his own accord. He admitted he lied to the police, as he had consistently done over nine visits to Leighton Buzzard police station.

There could never be any doubt among the jury of ten men and two women that Stone killed Ruby Keen. The question was: was it in circumstances amounting to murder or manslaughter? The defence maintained there was no malice aforethought. They retired, and

RUBY KEEN MURDER TRIAL

HEATH LABOURER AT THE OLD BAILEY

HEARING-ADJOURNED

The Ruby Keen murder trial opened before the Lord-Chief
Justice (Lord Hewart) at the Old Bailey yesterday (Monday).

Leslie George Stone (24), labourer, of Heath-and-Reach, was
charged with the murder of Ruby Annie Keen (23), a factory
worker of Plantation Road, Leighton Buzzard, whose body was
found on the Fire footpath near her home, on April 12th.

Mr. Richard O'Sullivan, K.C., and Mr. Christmas Humphreys
conducted the case for the Crown, and Stone was represented by
Mr. Maurice Healy, K.C., and Mr. C. L. Henderson, instructed by
Messrs. Thornley & Boutwood, of Leighton Buzzard.

A coach was reserved on the 8.25 a.m. train from Leighton
Buzzard to London for the 47 witnesses who were expected to
give evidence. These included policemen, bar tenders and factory

Cutting from the Leighton Buzzard Observer, 29 June, 1937

came back with a question for the judge. 'If, as the result of an
intention to commit rape, the girl was killed although there was no
intention to kill her, is a man guilty of murder?' The judge replied,
'Yes, undoubtedly.' After consulting the other jury members for a

moment, the foreman passed their unanimous verdict: 'Guilty'.

This was an astonishing end to the trial. Until the question about 'an intention to commit rape', there had been no mention of any sexual motive by Stone, although one was always implied. Although Ruby Keen was left partly stripped with her legs spreadeagled, with the knee-prints of her killer between her legs, 'rape' had simply not featured on anyone's agenda. There is no record of whether or not her knickers had been removed. And yet, at the eleventh hour, and of their own volition, the lay members of the jury wanted to know about 'an intention to commit rape'. And the judge, none other than the Lord Chief Justice himself, simply told them, 'Yes, undoubtedly.' Guilty of murder then!

There was an appeal against the conviction, but not directly over this point. Instead, in a labyrinth of technical law, the defence maintained the judge had misdirected the jury, saying that his reply to their question of 'rape' was inadequate to enable the jury to reach a correct verdict in law.

A man could not be guilty of crime, they said, unless he had put it out of his power to withdraw from the completion of the crime. There was always a *locus paenitentiae*, room for penitence. The matter had to be approached from the aspect of the crime — attempted rape or assault, presumably — for which the appellant would have been convicted if the girl had not died as the result of the assault. The maximum offence for which he could have been convicted if she had not died would have been assault with intent to commit rape or attempted rape, both misdemeanours (not felonies). In such a case, where death was unintentional, the crime could not be murder. The Lord Chief Justice ought to have asked the jury to consider whether they thought Stone ought to have known that his act must have resulted in at least grievous bodily harm. The answer given to the jury was not adequate and was a 'grave misdirection'. So argued Stone's defence.

The appeal judge said a most wicked, cruel and violent assault had been made on the dead woman. No-one could doubt the object had been to ravish her. (One would have thought someone would have said so during the trial). If a man intended to rape a woman but without the intention to kill her, if he had had squeezed her by the throat in order to overpower her and in doing so killed her, this amounted to murder. Quite so. The appeal was dismissed. Leslie George Stone was hanged at Pentonville at 8 o'clock on Friday, 13th August, 1937. At the time of his execution a service for his family was held in his home at Heath and Reach. As in all cases, there is more than one victim when it comes to murder. And hanging too, for that matter.

The Verdict

It seems incredible that an intention by Leslie George Stone to rape Ruby Keen, if he had such intention, was not a major feature at his trial. Since it was not, who is to say rape or sexual assault was on his mind at all? Maybe they were about to make consensual love in a lovers' lane when they quarrelled, as he said. Maybe she was willing to have sex, and was lying on her back with him between her legs when it all went wrong. They had both been drinking. Who knows what happened? We might have known if the prosecution had brought 'rape' into it. Now we'll never know.

But whatever happened, Leslie Stone killed her. He knotted her scarf so tight around her neck and left her on the ground to die within three minutes. Whether there was an attempt to rape or not, he murdered Ruby Keen.

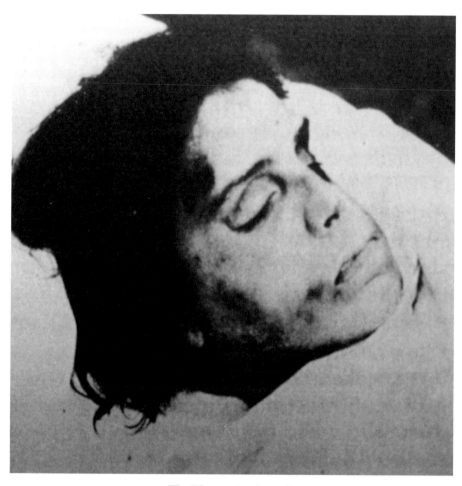

The Woman in the sack
She was identified as Mrs Caroline Manton

Luton 1943—44

The Body in the Sack

If, for any reason, scenes of crime officers attended your house and made a thorough examination for fingerprints, would you expect them to find any? Of course you would, for don't you routinely touch and pick things up at home? Cups and saucers, magazines, door handles, table tops and countless other things — your fingerprints will be everywhere. Yet when police visited a house in Regent Street, Luton, in February, 1944, the address of Mr and Mrs Manton and their four children, they found no fingerprints, bar one, on an old pickle jar in a cupboard below the stairs. How strange.

This is a tale of murder, followed by a determined and cunning attempt to avoid detection. Only persistence, coupled with the tad of good fortune police need in such cases, enabled the killer to be brought to justice. The same good fortune also enabled his victim to be identified, which is why fingerprint evidence was vital in this case.

The story begins on Friday, 19th November, 1943, when two sewer men were walking along the banks of the River Lea, Luton, testing water levels. The path they trod was used by locals and employees of the nearby Vauxhall motor works. The men noticed a sack in the river and decided to investigate. What until then would have been an ordinary, uneventful day changed completely when they discovered its contents — the naked body of a dead woman. Her ankles had been tied together, and her knees were bound to her stomach by a cord tied about her waist. Her face was battered out of recognition. Her teeth had been removed and there was no jewellery or any other identifying features.

It was clear that her killer had taken all possible steps to ensure she could not be identified. The Home Office pathologist, Dr Keith Simpson, attended the scene and declared the woman to be about 35 years old, had worn false teeth and had had at least one child. She was pregnant. She was 5 feet 5 inches tall with dark hair. She had been strangled, but not before sustaining a blow to the head which had fractured her jaw and caused haemorrhaging in the brain. She was calculated to have been dead for about eighteen hours. As was custom in those days, the local police called in Scotland Yard, who dispatched Detective Chief Inspector Chapman to Luton.

It was vital to identify the body. Without knowing who the woman was, or where she came from, where could the police make a start on detecting the crime? There seemed a good possibility that she was local, so to assist with identification the woman's face was 'rebuilt' to look as far as possible as she did before she was beaten out of recognition, then photographed and shown to the public. Her features appeared in newspapers and even on cinema screens. Later, it was discovered that her 17-year-old daughter and two of her teenage sons, despite seeing the pictures, failed to recognise their own mother. Her fingerprints were taken and checked with those on file, without any breakthrough.

Police checked missing persons files, in the process tracing a number of missing women. They failed to identify the body in the sack. They interviewed staff and lorry drivers at the Vauxhall works, to no avail. A plaster cast of the woman's jaw was made and shown to local dentists, but they were unable to help. They visited laundries to see if anyone had failed to collect any garments, but without success. They discovered a local dealer supplied sacks like the one in which the woman's body was found, but they were not individually identifiable and he kept no records. The string, or cord, used to bind her was commonplace and could have been acquired anywhere. They checked out male service personnel (this was wartime Britain) whose women friends had not responded to their letters. They searched dustbins, refuse tips. They did house to house enquiries, showing the picture of the mystery woman. Their every turn met a dead end.

Then, in February, 1944, still searching, or possibly re-searching, police found a fragment of cloth among household rubbish on a council tip. Attached to it was what appeared to be a dry cleaner's label, bearing the number: V12247. This was traced to Sketchley Dye Works, Wellington Street, Luton. The shop records showed this to be a coat handed in for dyeing the previous November by Mrs Caroline Manton, Regent Street, Luton. The picture of the dead woman's face had been shown at every house there, but no-one had recognised her.

One imagines the Scotland Yard detectives wasted no time in knocking on the door of the Manton household. Mr Manton was not at home. When police spoke to a neighbour she explained that she had not seen Mrs Manton for some time, but she understood she was away, visiting her mother. When they knocked again the door was opened by the Mantons' 17-year-old daughter who said her mother was not at home but her father was. He was Horace William Manton, alias Bertie, aged 40, a driver-fireman. He said he and his wife hadn't been getting on and that she was always mixing with soldiers. He said a midwife who was attending to his pregnant wife had received a note apparently signed by her saying she had gone to Grantham, to her brother's, and her mother had received letters, too, all posted in North London after the mystery woman's body had been found.

Manton was shown the picture, but denied it was his wife. It couldn't be, he said, referring to the letters as proof. Sure enough, North London postmarks supported his story. They purported to have been written by his wife, and contained a Hampstead address. Clearly, if this was so, the dead woman was not his wife. The postmarks could not lie. But did Mrs Manton write the letters?

The police had the dead woman's fingerprints. They would know if she and Mrs Manton were one and the same when they made an examination of the Manton household. But this was inconclusive, for there were no fingerprints to be found — except one. On an old pickle jar in a cupboard below the stairs, out of sight and long out of mind, one fingerprint was found. It matched one of the prints of the

Body In Sack Said To Be Now Identified As A Luton Woman

Husband Arrested And Charged With Murder

The Luton "sack" mystery came into new prominence yesterday with the news that the identity of the victim had been established and a charge of murder preferred at Luton Borough Court against her husband, who was described as a fireman.

Accused, Bertie Horace William Manton, aged 40, of 14, Regent-street, Luton, was charged with murdering Irene Caroline Seagrave Manton at Luton on November 18.

After brief evidence he was remanded in custody until Wednesday week, March 8.

Mrs. Manton was the mother of four children, two of them over 14 and the other, aged

dead woman. She was Irene Caroline Seagrave Manton.

Meanwhile, Detective Inspector Chapman was examining those letters. Posted in North London, yes. Written by Caroline Manton, impossible. Unless she did so before her death and they were posted weeks later, unlikely. There was one striking feature in the handwriting: Hampstead was incorrectly spelt as 'Hamstead', with no letter 'p'. Manton was asked to write the name. He did so, spelling it with no letter 'p'. He had written the letters himself. The case was secured by police finding notepaper at the Manton home, which matched that of the letters supposedly sent by Mrs Manton, and they also established the coat which had been dyed black was so that Mrs Manton could wear it at a funeral.

Bertie Manton confessed to killing his wife. He said he had lost his temper after discovering she had been in the local pubs with soldiers. He made a statement, in which he said he struck her on the head with a wooden stool, causing her to fall backwards and onto the floor. He had not meant to kill her, but when he realised he had he decided to get rid of her body. He undressed her, took some sacks from the cellar, which he cut up then tied her up in them and took her body down into the cellar. He washed away the blood and hid her bloodstained clothes. After having tea with the children, he went out into the darkness provided by the 'blackout' and he took his wife's body to the river over the handlebars of his bicycle.

His story, if true, might have secured a conviction for manslaughter, since he implied that he had not expressly intended to kill her. But Caroline Manton had been strangled. Dr Simpson told the jury she had been gripped about the throat and struck with a blunt instrument – not quite the same as being struck by a stool in the way Manton had described. He was convicted of murder and sentenced to death. His sentence was commuted to life imprisonment and he served just three years before dying in prison in 1947.

Heath and Reach 1882

Without Malice Aforethought

A 'build-up' of domestic incidents often provides warning of things to come which, if not acted upon, might have tragic consequences. A 19th century case at Heath and Reach was tragic, a hapless wife killed in her bed as she slept, by a husband who was no longer in charge of his own mind.

George and Mary Ann Battams, aged 65 and 55 respectively, lived in a small cottage. They had ten sons, five of whom lived at home. In those typically Victorian days, the house was overcrowded, the parents occupying a bedroom downstairs, their sons in another upstairs. About 6.15 a.m. on Saturday, 6th May, 1882, as she slept in her bed, Mary Ann was brutally attacked by her husband who struck her repeatedly about the head with a billhook, a heavy tool with a sharply pointed end. Dr Bodger found her lying 'in clotted blood' from a wound on the right side of her head with the brain protruding, and about five other wounds about her head. She was alive but 'in a state of collapse'.

Mrs Battams' screams were heard by her son, Joseph Battams, 15. He ran downstairs to find his mother still on her bed, bleeding from her wounds. His father was standing nearby in his shirt, holding the billhook. He called for his brothers, and asked his father what he had done. 'I didn't know I was doing anything,' he replied, then he broke down in tears. Later, he told PC Cook, 'She aggravated me. She called me a devil.' Mary Ann lived until the Monday, when she opened her eyes and saw her family around her before passing away.

Charged with murder, George Battams appeared at the Midsummer Assizes at Bedford. John Battams, Joseph's older brother, said, 'He could not have been in his right mind when he did it, and I hope you will look upon him' (meaning to show him mercy).

Heath and Reach
Home of George and Mary Battams

Superintendent Shepherd told the court that George Battams had complained about his head and had not been able to work. Mrs Battams went out charring. George wanted her to stay at home and look after him, but she would not. One supposes she went to work to earn money, which George was unable to do. On the day before he killed her she had threatened to leave him. The next morning, at five o'clock, he said he wanted her to stay at home that day. She said she would not. He took the billhook and hit her on the head with it. John Battams said that his mother was younger and stronger than George and could have defended herself, so she must have been struck when she was asleep.

Mr F. Pilgrim, a surgeon, said he had professionally attended to George Battams for eight months prior to the murder. He had rheumatism and was unable to work as a labourer. He said that George had complained of severe pains in the head, irritability, sleepless nights and depression. He seemed to think the world was against him. Mr Pilgrim noted that the brain is always associated with insanity, so that there is a 'softening' of it. In his opinion George was of unsound mind due to having brain disease.

Shortly before the murder George Battams went into the workhouse, where he received medical attention. But he wanted to go home. He was released, with the recommendation that he go to the infirmary where he could be looked after. Instead, his wife said she would look after him. Other witnesses testified to George's complaints about his head, his restlessness, hearing noises and depression. The jury acquitted him on the grounds of insanity without retiring. He was detained 'during Her Majesty's Pleasure'. It is such a pity he did not receive the medical treatment and care he so obviously needed. This was Victorian England. It couldn't happen today. Could it?

10

Little Staughton 1870–71

The Killing of Old Sally

'An imbecile woman who had been under medical supervision as a lunatic, living in her isolated cottage. Irritable in disposition and possessed of some undefined dread that she was about to be turned out, she was in the habit of screaming out at the slightest provocation. The youth of the village took mischievous delight in throwing stones at her door and subjecting her to annoyance, so that few neighbours within earshot of her cries ceased to take notice of them either by day or night'. So it was that just before midnight of Tuesday, 29th November, 1870, in her cottage at Little Staughton, when 51-year-old Sarah Marshall was heard to scream, no-one took the slightest notice. She was known as Old Sally and she had been brutally murdered.

Giving evidence at the inquest at the Shoulder of Mutton public house, Mary Hawkins said she was in bed when she heard knocking at Old Sally's door, followed by a scream. It was nearly midnight, she said, for soon after her clock struck the hour. James and Susan Criswell were in bed too when they heard rapping at Sally's door, followed by a scream. Of the time they were uncertain, as their clock did not work. No-one took any notice, because Sally was always 'hollering', even at night.

Sally was seen alive and well at her cottage at nine o'clock on Tuesday evening by her nephew's wife, Jane Marshall. The cottage was a one-roomed cabin. It stood on wasteland by the roadside. A narrow strip of ground, accessed by a stile, led to her front door. At the back was a ditch and hedge and beyond that a ploughed field.

About a quarter to eight the next day – the morning after the scream – Sally's niece, Emma Caris, called at Mr Gray's grocer's shop. He said, 'Just ask who was out so late last night', meaning go and enquire about Sally's welfare. After climbing the stile, she discovered the front door was open slightly. She pushed it open further, and discovered the feet of her aunt hanging over the bedstead. She called out to Mr Gray, 'Oh dear, someone has killed Sally.' Mr Gray saw Sally, still in her night-dress, with her feet hanging over the bottom of the bedstead, and that one of the laths, or slats, had given way so that her body was 'sunk down', its back resting on the floor. He said she must have been forced through the bed. There was a little blood on the floor close to the body. He locked up the cottage and went for Constable Sturges.

PC Sturges examined the scene and searched for a weapon, finding none. He secured the cottage and made an examination outside. He found a gap in the hedge at the rear where he discovered footprints made by nailed shoes. They were pointing away from the cottage, towards the field. He saw two impressions made by the knees of corduroy trousers in the soil at the top of the bank, which was about 3 feet high, together with the impressions of someone's knuckles.

Dr Hemming attended also. He arrived at the cottage about noon. He found Sally's body to be cold and stiff, with her knees bent. There were no penetrating wounds in her head, chest or abdomen. Her tongue protruded from her mouth. She might have died naturally, except she had been forced through the laths and the doctor discovered irregular bruises on the throat, with scratches and lacerations. There were severe bruises and lacerations on the back of her right shoulder, on the back of her right arm and on her elbows and wrists. There were more severe bruises on the lower part of the back, as if caused by many blows. There had been bleeding from the anus. The arms were crossed and the fingers were clenched. He believed death to have been caused by strangulation.

He made a post mortem examination and was able to say that the wound to the anus, together with the wounds inflicted on the back of the deceased, was caused by a blunt-pointed instrument. Someone had attacked Old Sally and jabbed her repeatedly and with great force in the back, and at some point thrust the 'instrument' into her. Something the shape of a broom handle, perhaps. The attack as a whole seemed to form some sort of deliberate torture before she was strangled. Who would have done such a thing? And why?

Dr Hemming examined clothing belonging to a suspect. These consisted of a pair of corduroy trousers, two 'slop' (loose) jackets and a shirt. All had red stains on them, in the case of one of the slops near the wrist. The stains appeared to be blood, and an attempt had been made to wash it out. He would be able to say that it was either human or mammals' blood.

Nine o'clock wasn't the last time Old Sally was believed to have been alive. A shepherd, Joseph Green, happened to pass by Sally's cottage, apparently sometime between 10 and 11 o'clock, when he saw a man standing on the road close to the stile. He had his back towards him. Green said 'Goodnight' as he passed and the man did not reply. He said he appeared to be wearing a slop, corduroy trousers and a cap. He could not identify him but took him to be William Bull. Green said the night was a dark one, so how he could say that the man wore corduroys, and why he thought he was William Bull when he did not recognise him you might wonder. Fitting the bill comes to mind, for by the time he testified police had their suspect.

Green also said that when he was about 40 yards from the cottage he heard a noise as if the door was being undone, or maybe it was a knock. He then heard a woman's voice say, 'I always pay my rent as well as you do. You have been here once before tonight.' He heard no other voice.

In making early enquiries to identify the killer, it wasn't long before the police had a name. Billy Bull, as he was known locally, lived in Little Staughton and was everybody's favourite suspect. He was 22 years old. On the night of the murder he had spent four hours or so drinking at Wildman's beerhouse in the village with Jonathan Smith. They had left about 10.15 and walked together in the direction of Bushmead, towards Smith's house. This was away from the direction of Bull's house where he lived with his mother.

About one o'clock the day after the murder PC Sturges saw Bull in a field, chaff-cutting. In the presence of others the officer asked him, 'Where were you last night?' Bull: 'What do you want to know for?' The officer told him. Bull: 'I was at Wildman's (beerhouse).' Bull said he left between nine and ten with Jonathan Smith and that they walked towards Smith's house together. They met Jim Maddison and a man called Stapleton on the road and chatted. Then he went home. The officer had nothing to go on then, but about 11 p.m. that night he again went to see Bull, this time at his home. He was not there. The following morning he returned and still he was not there. On the Friday, just after midnight, he found Bull at home. He told him he was taking him into custody on suspicion of murder. Bull had other ideas. He fled.

The officer pursued him and caught him, and after a struggle he was handed over to Superintendent Sharnbrook and examined. Bull was wearing a slop jacket and corduroy trousers, a flat cap and nailed boots. There was blood on his clothing which he, Bull, accounted for in the following statement: 'I was rat catching. That's what caused the blood, I'm sure. I went along the road on Tuesday night with Smith and left him at Willow-row End. I met Maddison there and went home a little after ten. I went to bed. I never came out again that night'.

Sarah Barleman told the inquest Sally used to come to her shop once a week. Sally had mentioned boys throwing stones at her door saying, 'One day they will kill me.' 'Do they come in and meddle with

PETTY SESSIONS, Tuesday, Dec. 20.

Before the Hon. St. Andrew St. John (chairman) ;
Sir Salisbury G. Payne, Bart. ; the Rev. C. C. Beaty-
Pownall ; and C. Magniac, Esq., M.P.

THE MURDER AT LITTLE STAUGHTON.

William Bull, labourer, of Little Staughton, who
had been apprehended on suspicion of causing the
death of Sarah Marshall, at Little Staughton, under
circumstances already fully described in these columns,
was placed in the dock to-day on the same charge.

The prisoner was conveyed from Bedford Gaol by
Mr. Deputy Chief Constable Graham, and throughout
the proceedings manifested great interest in the evidence, the blood occasionally mounting to his cheeks
and suffusing his whole face as any allusion was made
which seemed to connect him with the crime.

The Chief Constable of the County, Captain E. M.
Boultbee, was present during the day.

The prosecution was conducted by Mr. W. A.
Stimson ; the prisoner had no professional advice.
The following is a full report of the evidence :—

Jane Marshall deposed : I am the wife of James
Marshall and live at Little Staughton. I knew the
deceased, who was no relation to me, but was related
to my husband. last saw her alive on

A newspaper cutting, the Little Staughton murder

you,' she was asked. 'Yes they do,' she replied. 'Bull came in the other night and I took the broom to him. He took it away and hit me over the arms with it.'

At William Bull's trial, in March, 1871, it was noted that 'the court was densely crowded, with some ladies being present throughout'. Prosecution counsel opened by describing Sally Marshall as 'what most people would call a half-witted creature not having the ordinary amount of sense other people are blessed with'. This may have been accurate, but it was hardly Bull's fault and was not evidence against him.

Dr Hemming reiterated the testimony he had given at the inquest, adding that the body of Sally Marshall had been pulled up onto the bed when he arrived at the cottage (by others who had visited the scene before he got there). He said the bruising to her back, her shoulders and the backs of her hands and elbows were caused by a blunt instrument, and that none of the lacerations punctured the skin. A penetrating wound had been made into her anus, forcing its way through tissues of flesh, forwards, perhaps by the handle of a common stick, and with great violence. The wound 'tore forwards neatly to the sexual parts'. It seems Sally was forced to lie on her front and was jabbed repeatedly into her back passage. Death was by strangulation after. There was no doubt that there had been an attempt to wash the blood from Bull's clothing. Whether the blood was human or animal he could not say. He said that Bull suffered from an itch that would have caused him to scratch himself, perhaps drawing his own blood.

Jonathan Smith, Bull's friend, confirmed that he and Bull, together with Wildman, had caught about sixty rats, 'pulling them from their holes'. They killed them by hitting their heads on to their boots. Jack Stapleton, whom Bull and Smith met on the road after leaving the beerhouse, said that when they and Jim Maddison chatted on the road, Bull said he 'was of a good mind to go and call Old Sally up and make a to-do.' Maddison said, 'Let the poor old creature alone. Let her rest.' Bull denied any such conversation.

Another man, Frederick Darlow, said that the previous month he and others, including William Bull, left the Shoulder of Mutton and nearing Old Sally's Bull picked up a stone and threw it at her door. Sally cried out, 'Murder!' and 'Damn you!' Enza Wagstaffe said she knew Old Sally, whom she said told her Bull would kill her, and that she had spoken of his violent conduct. Dr Hemming said that Sally would cry 'Murder' to anyone who happened to be passing.

At the trial, the jury was told that although Bull had previously threatened Sally, they had to deal with the evidence they had before them. All the young men in the parish had 'subjected her to annoyance'. As to the witness, Green, he had not identified Bull, despite stating that he had 'known him all his life'. If he had not recognised him, and the man did not speak, how could he say he was the man he saw by Sally's cottage? The doctor was unable to say if the blood was a man's blood, a woman's blood or the blood of rats. Sadly, they did not have the forensic expertise of today. The wounds were caused by a stick. No-one had seen Bull carrying a stick, nor noticed that his clothes were bloodstained for that matter. No stick was found. On the matter of 'paying rent', Sally was always going on about this. It was irrelevant as far as the attack upon her was concerned. Strangely, no mention is made of Bull's mother, and whether or not she could confirm the time of his arrival home, that is if she knew it, or of his demeanour. Some suggestion was made by the prosecution that the motive for the attack was sexual, but there was no sign that Sally had been raped.

The evidence was circumstantial, all of it. One might just as well nominate the shepherd, Joseph Green, as a suspect. Couldn't he have called at Sally's that night, and couldn't he have thrown in the name of William Bull, whom he might have seen on the road, as a man seen loitering near her cottage? He named him yet said he could not recognise him, very strange, you might think.

It seems the most damning part laid at William Bull's door as far as the jury was concerned was that when he left the beerhouse with Smith he walked away from his own house, which was just 800 yards from Sally's. By the time he and Smith parted on the road he had 1,020 yards to walk home. This, after a session in the beerhouse and the alleged comments about looking old Sally up, denied by Bull, must have been enough to persuade the jury. They took just twenty minutes to return a verdict of Guilty. The judge told him, 'Prepare to die, as you have no chance of mercy in this world.' Bull listened with stolid indifference and had nothing to say. Unlike others condemned to die, no-one campaigned to have his sentence commuted. Even those opposed to capital punishment were silent. William Bull's savage assault and murder of a harmless woman in her own home, for it was he, met with no sympathy from any quarter.

The Verdict

There was no proof that William Bull murdered Sally Marshall. He was not positively identified at the scene. Blood grouping was impossible, and the blood found on Bull's clothing could not even be classified as human. No 'contamination' evidence was available. He had shown aggression and made threats to her, but so had others. There were imprints of corduroy trousers in the ground at the back of Sally's house, but such garments were worn by most of the labouring classes. There was no obvious motive for the crime. He made no admission. A case must be proved 'beyond reasonable doubt', especially where someone will forfeit their life if found guilty. This case was not. By nothing more than chance, the verdict was correct. On his own admissions, made later to the governor in Bedford jail, William Bull was guilty.

The Execution of William Bull

At 8 a.m. on Monday, 3rd April, 1871, William Bull was executed at Bedford prison on the same scaffold as William Worsley and Joseph Castle before him, the 'engine of death' as it was described. His executioner was Calcraft. Following an instruction by the Home Secretary that the bell of the nearest church to a prison must toll at an execution, the sound of the bells of Holy Trinity could be heard, alongside the prison bell itself.

When Bull stepped from his cell to the landing to be pinioned he was calm enough. He remained so on the journey down the stone staircase towards the scaffold, accompanied by warders, the chaplain and others, and the press. No longer were the public permitted to witness an execution, but they could read all about it afterwards. As the procession emerged from the front door Bull's demeanour changed as tears flowed down his cheeks – tears of penitence, it was reported, and not tears of mental depression, although how anyone could know is impossible to imagine. His step remained firm, although this gave way to some unsteadiness when he caught sight of the scaffold.

He knelt in prayer with the chaplain, then shook hands with the prison governor and even Calcraft before climbing onto the scaffold. He was seen to look upward one last time before the white cap was placed upon his head, the noose about his neck and the trapdoor sprung. It is reported that he died instantaneously. The black flag was raised to signify to those outside, some seven hundred strong, that the sentence had been carried out and that a guilty man had been punished.

For William Bull was guilty. He admitted his crime in two signed confessions, taken down in prison by the governor, at his dictation, as he awaited death. The first went part-way only to the whole truth. He admitted throwing a stone at Old Sally's door on the night in

125

question, saying when she opened the door she swore at him as he stood in the middle of the road. 'I went into the house and she called me a hen roost robber'. He could not recall whether she was dressed or in her night-dress. He left after two or three minutes. He said that after he threw the stone she came out with a long sweeping broom, struck him with it and the head of the broom came off. He said the last time she 'hot' me (hit me) he knocked her down, and that he was in a rage. She was lying on the bricks (laths) when he left. She was swearing at him and she was not dead. He never used the stick on her.

A few days later two of his sisters visited him and implored him to 'make peace with his Maker'. The governor said that he must tell the whole truth. The next day he made his second statement, a summary of which reads thus:

'When I left the beerhouse on the night of the murder Jonathan Smith was with me. I parted with him at Willow-row End.' He saw Maddison and Stapleton, and they spoke about getting work and Old Sally. 'Don't meddle with the old girl, not tonight,' he was urged. His route home took him past Old Sally's door. He pelted her door with stones. She stood in the doorway and swore at him and when he approached she struck at him with the broom. The head fell off. She went inside, he followed and she struck him with the broom handle. The room was in darkness, 'without fire or light'. He struck her with his right hand, knocking her to the floor. They struggled and he got hold of her throat with his left hand to prevent her from screaming. 'I tried to have connexion with her,' he added, almost as an afterthought.

He went outside to see if anyone was about, then returned and seized her throat again and punched her as hard as he could. 'I picked her up, took hold of one arm and one leg and whacked her on the bed.' She was 'quite dead'. 'I never used any stick,' he said. He tried to climb through the hedge at the back of the house to go home, but could not so he went over the stile instead. He had beer that night but was not drunk. His mother was up when he got home. He did not think it was yet eleven o'clock. He saw Joseph Green, the shepherd, who had a dog with him. It was the dog, not Green, he recognised.

The truth, then, or almost. He did not admit the atrocity with the stick, or broom handle as it probably was. Maybe shame prevented him from doing so. He did admit to sexual intent. This was an attempt to rape as well as a murder. Shame probably played a part in his reluctance to admit that too.

James Hanratty

II

Deadman's Hill — the A6 Murder

James Hanratty:
Beyond Reasonable Doubt?

Hanratty. For over forty years his name has been associated with murder, not only because of the crime he allegedly committed, but also the relentless campaign to prove his innocence, and that his conviction was a miscarriage of justice. Which is ironic, as the name derives from the Irish, meaning 'descendant of the lawyer'.

The crimes, for there were more than one, were brutal. But for the grace of God, there would have been two murders: the death of an innocent man, a woman raped and shot five times and left for dead at the roadside. It was never going to be an easy case for the police to crack. Crack it they did, in terms of arrest and conviction of the alleged killer. The case against Hanratty was built on an amazing coincidence, and a few others besides, over the series of events that began in Buckinghamshire, traversed other areas and ended up in Bedfordshire, and subsequent police enquiries in London. It was the Bedfordshire Constabulary who had responsibility, at first, for the investigation. In those days, however, when a murder was committed in the provinces, it was normal to call in 'the Yard', who had greater expertise and resources (not because they were better detectives). I have tried to outline events as they occurred. It isn't possible to fit all the detail into these pages.

Events began on a summer's evening, Tuesday, 22nd August,

1961, at Taplow, a small village in south Buckinghamshire. Michael Gregsten, 36, who lived with his wife and two sons at Abbots Langley, near Watford, was having an affair with Valerie Storie, 22. They had met in the canteen at a local research laboratory where they both worked as civil servants, and had been seeing one another for some time. It had been a typical day: Gregsten had taken his sons to play in Cassiobury Park, Watford, and after taking them home he told his wife, Janet, who was aware of the relationship, that he was off to see Valerie.

Gregsten had a Morris Minor car, grey colour. He and Storie went to their regular haunt, the Old Station Inn, Taplow, leaving after nine o'clock. They then drove to a cornfield at Dorney Reach, by the Thames, and parked. It was dusk. As they sat talking, a man tapped on the driver's window and when Gregston wound it down he said, 'This is a hold-up. I am a desperate man.' The man got into the back seat behind Gregsten and pointed a gun, which he said was loaded, at his head. The man wore a handkerchief around the bottom half of his face.

The man robbed the couple of their watches and made Gregsten hand over his wallet, containing £3, and Storie her purse, which had contained £7, but she sneaked the money into her bra without the man noticing. There was much conversation between the parties, until finally the man said he wanted something to eat. He told Gregsten to start driving.

At gunpoint, Gregston drove. One can imagine it, the three of them in the little Morris Minor on quiet roads — as they were then. They drove through Slough, called for petrol near Heathrow airport, drove on through Greenford, Harrow, Watford and St Albans. At one point Gregston flashed his reversing lights to try and attract attention. This caused a car to pull up alongside, the occupants making gestures towards the rear, whereupon Gregston and the man got out to check the rear lights. Valerie Storie could have fled, but would not leave her lover to the mercy of the gunman.

Eventually, they drove up the A6 into Bedfordshire. At Deadman's Hill, south of Bedford, the man told Gregston to park in a layby on the other side of the road and turn off the lights. It was well after midnight. The man said he wanted to 'kip' — a word that would feature later when Hanratty was interviewed by police — and he decided to tie up his captives. There was a duffel bag by Storie's feet. The man told Gregsten to give it to him, possibly hoping to find cord or something. Gregsten picked it up and thrust it over his shoulder towards the man, too forcefully perhaps. Whatever, the man shot Gregsten twice through the head. Valerie Storie would later say she could 'hear the blood'. 'He moved too quick,' the man said, and they sat there for twenty minutes with Gregsten dead in the driving seat.

A little later the man asked Storie to kiss him. She refused, but at gunpoint she got into the back of the car where she succumbed to sexual intercourse, which in these circumstances amounted to rape. Later still she had to help the man drag Gregsten's body from the vehicle, after which he asked her how to start the car and to *show him how it worked*. He then shot her 5 times, at one point calmly reloading the gun, then drove off, leaving her for dead. At 6.30 a.m. she was found by a farm labourer, who heard her groaning. He went down the road and told John Kerr, 18, who was conducting a traffic survey at the roadside. Kerr flagged down a passing motorist. An ambulance and the police were called. Storie lived, but she had been shot through the spine and was paralysed from the neck down. She would never walk again. Police took possession of her clothing and took samples, in keeping with the rape allegation.

Valerie Storie gave police a description of the attacker. How accurate it would have been you may question, given that events took place in darkness and the gunman was sat in the back seat of the car, apart from when he raped her, also in darkness. But she did say that at one point, in the layby, she saw his face lit up by the headlights of a passing car. He had staring eyes, she said. And she had heard him speak. He had a London accent. Police issued a photofit. It would have been useless, surely. The Yard was called in. Detective Superintendent Acott was in charge.

At 7.10 that morning the Morris Minor was seen being driven erratically in Redbridge, north-east London. The gunman, remember, had asked Valerie Storie to show him how the car worked, which suggested he could not drive. Witnesses saw the driver's face. The car was found abandoned that evening, in Redbridge. The next day, a startling discovery: at 8.45 p.m. a revolver and sixty rounds of ammunition, wrapped in a white handkerchief, were found hidden behind the back seat on the top deck of a number 36A bus, in the depot at Peckham, London. It was confirmed as the murder weapon. There were no fingerprints.

Police made a routine appeal to hotels and guesthouses, asking: 'Landladies, do you have a lodger...?' They received an interesting reply from an hotel in Finsbury Park. Guests were suspicious of a man called Frederick Durrant, of Sussex. The name and address proved to be false, so the police took him in. He admitted he was Peter Louis Alphon, of Streatham. He said he used a false name because he sometimes left hotels without paying his bill. The police found a newspaper cutting of the A6 murder in his case. On the day of the murder he had stayed in Room 6 at the Vienna Hotel, a dosshouse, in Maida Vale, north London. Alphon was released 'pending enquiries'. On 11th September two spent cartridges cases were discovered in Room 24 of the same hotel. They were both confirmed as having been fired by the murder weapon.

This turn of events — a chance call following an appeal concerning Peter Alphon, and subsequently the discovery of the two cartridges, would lead directly to the arrest of James Hanratty. For, according to the hotel register, Room 24, where the cartridges were found, was occupied on 21st August — the day before the murder — by one J. Ryan who, as the police would discover, was Hanratty.

First, though, we must deal with Peter Alphon, whom the police reasonably considered was their man. The hotel manager, a dubious character called William Nudds, and his equally dubious 'wife', Florence Snell, had provided Alphon with an alibi, saying he was at the Vienna at 11 p.m. on the day of the murder. The police, convinced he was the killer, took new statements, in which both persons rescinded their first statements and now stated that Alphon had not returned to the hotel by 2 a.m. They said that he had visited Room 24 before taking Room 6. Alphon was placed on an identification parade where Valerie Storie 'identified' another man, not him, as the murderer. The case against Alphon collapsed, so the police took a third statement from Nudds and Snell, in which they changed their statements again saying the first were true after all — that Alphon *was* at the hotel and therefore had an alibi. In fact, checking his alibi proved to be difficult if not impossible. Nudds had at least eight or nine (or more) other names. The man was utterly unreliable.

So now, having had their prime suspect apparently eliminated, the police had to find someone else. They turned their attention to J. Ryan. How they ever discovered that he was James Hanratty was never established. But he was.

James Francis Hanratty was born in London 4th October, 1936. His father was Irish, his mother came from Durham. James first got into trouble with the law at 17, when he stole a motorcycle. He graduated to housebreaking (burglary) and stealing cars. Inevitably, he ended up in prison, from which he tried to escape more than once. He had no 'form' for violence. As it happened, he was wanted by the police for housebreaking, identified by his fingerprints at the scene of the crime. Not a man for wearing gloves, then.

On 7th September Hanratty was in Ireland, where his car was in collision with another driven, astonishingly, by someone from Sarratt, Hertfordshire, not far from Gregsten's home. When Hanratty got wind that he was a suspect for the A6 murder, through his father (who had been told by the press), he went straight to the top and telephoned Supt Acott. He told him he did not do the A6 murder. In another call he confirmed that he had stayed at the Vienna Hotel on the 21st (the day before the murder) for one night. Then, he said, he went to Liverpool to stay with friends. He would not tell Supt Acott who they were (one of them was wanted by the police).

Hanratty was talking to the police, but not face to face. He soon would be. On 11th October two policemen in Blackpool noticed a young man drinking coffee in a café and waited for him outside. The man said he was Peter Bates, but the officers were not fooled. They had just detained Britain's most wanted man, James Hanratty. He went on an identity parade at Bedfordshire HQ, where he was picked out by two of the witnesses who had seen the man driving the Morris Minor in Redbridge. Two others failed to identify him. Then they put him on another parade, this time in the ward at Stoke Mandeville Hospital, where Valerie Storie was being treated in the spinal injuries unit. After her earlier false identification it was vital she did not fail again.

Propped up in her hospital bed, she was pushed back and forth along the line of men. She picked out Hanratty as the man who had murdered her lover and who had raped and tried to murder her — not by sight, but by asking every person to say, 'Be quiet, will you, I am thinking', just as the man had done that night. Every man on the parade said it, and she chose Hanratty. Critics will point out she was bound to, since the lineup was formed of servicemen, taken from nearby bases, all from different parts of country, not from London. Taking into account that at an earlier parade she had identified the wrong man, and the conditions on the night of the crime — darkness and their positions in the Morris Minor — it must be assumed that Valerie Storie's identification was, through no fault of her own, next to worthless. The police would need more than the evidence of 'identification', such as it was, to prove the case against Hanratty. Nevertheless they charged him that night, even though they had just learned that none of the fingerprints found in the car were his.

Today's Rotary Club Site, Ampthill
Scene of Committal Proceedings of James Hanratty

If Hanratty could prove he was elsewhere at the time of the murder then obviously he was not the killer. Given that it was now about six weeks later, with a man like him who travelled and didn't exactly clock on at work, this would be difficult. How many of us can remember where we were six weeks ago, or even last week? In any event, he said that on the morning of the 22nd August he left the Vienna Hotel and took a bus to Liverpool, arriving between 4 and 6 p.m. He persisted with this account, even into his trial. He was lying, as he later admitted, probably to protect criminal friends (never mind his own life was on the line), or maybe because lying was always what he did. In this regard he did himself no good at all.

James Hanratty was tried for his life at the Shire Hall, Bedford, in January, 1962. The judge was Justice Gorman. The case was prosecuted by Graham Stanwick, and defended by Michael Sherrard. Hanratty faced the murder charge only; the attempted murder and rape of Valerie Storie were dropped. He pleaded 'not guilty'. He had not produced a confirmed alibi. What was the main thrust of the prosecution's evidence? Thrust was not the word.

Valerie Storie, testifying, said she had known Michael Gregsten since 1958 (about three years). They went motor rallying together. She said the man in the dock, Hanratty, was the gunman. He had staring eyes. She had no doubt, she said.

The evidence of identification was scant, to say the least. Of the witnesses, Storie had attended two identification parades, in the first picking out an innocent man, in the second picking out Hanratty by what he said in his Cockney accent. Two men had identified him as the driver of the car on the morning of the crime, but two had failed. The only forensic evidence of note was that the gunman was blood group O secretor, as was Hanratty, but so was 40% of the male population, including Alphon. They would be able to deduce blood grouping from semen, taken from Valerie Storie. This enabled them to rule out Gregsten as the man who had intercourse with her that night, as he was of another blood group. There was no forensic evidence and no fingerprints to link Hanratty to the crime. The recovered gun and ammunition could not be connected with him. The spent cartridges were recovered from the room in which he slept at the Vienna Hotel, but how long had they been there, hidden in the upholstery? How many others had slept in the room, and over what period?

Would 'J. Ryan', alias Hanratty, have come into the frame in the first place had not the police called at the Vienna Hotel to make enquires of another person entirely, Peter Alphon? Could Alphon be the killer even? The police, rightly, did everything in their power to secure conviction. That is their job, providing, of course, the evidence is fairly and diligently gathered. A serving prisoner, Roy Langdale, gave evidence to say Hanratty had confessed to him when they had been on remand, in Brixton. He was discredited after he admitted he had approached newspapers for payment for his story, and it seems much of what he alleged Hanratty had told him was either incorrect or could have been read in newspapers. Even so, he may have been telling the truth, that Hanratty had 'confessed'.

At the beginning of the second week of the trial, Hanratty said he had lied about his alibi. He had not been in Liverpool on the day of the murder: he had been in Rhyl, North Wales. Lying to one's own side, especially when your life is on the line, may seem a strange thing. But then, if he was innocent, he may have reasonably believed that surely no jury would believe he could be guilty, not in England where you get a fair trial. Or maybe, having lied about Liverpool, as he lied about most things, he felt he could not change his story, that to do so would make things worse. Or maybe he thought that even if he was in Rhyl, no-one could back him up.

Oh what a tangled web Hanratty weaved! Now his defence team had to dispatch someone to Rhyl to try and find someone who could support him, and be quick about it. Meanwhile, it was the turn of Supt Acott to take the stand. Apart from the usual flak police officers have to take from defence lawyers — and fair enough, it's their job to take it — there came a dispute over something Hanratty was alleged to have said. It concerned the work 'kip', meaning sleep. Acott said Hanratty had said 'sleep'. Hanratty said he had used the word 'kip'. The relevance of this would not be discovered until the case was reviewed nearly forty years later.

The prosecution alluded to part of Valerie Storie's statement, in which she had said the gunman had said 'call me Jim', suggesting this meant Jim as in James (Hanratty). The defence would argue he meant 'call me Jim' because Jim was anything but his real name. Point taken, in both respects. You couldn't have ruled out anyone, no matter what the gunman said. There was, of course, more evidence by other witnesses. Sherrard, for the defence, described the prosecution case as 'weak and shameful'.

Hanratty took the stand. He didn't have to. He could have said nothing at all, although the judge would have been obliged to comment to the jury. Something along the lines of 'would you believe someone is innocent if they say nothing?' He told the court that if he had wanted to do a 'stick up' he would not have gone to a cornfield, but to a bank or a shop. He accused Acott of omitting much of what he had said during interview, and adding things he had not said. (These were the days before tape recorded interviews). His alibi in Rhyl did not stand up, but that would not mean it was untrue. It simply could not be satisfactorily established.

The jury retired to consider their verdict. They returned after six hours, asking for advice on the meaning of 'reasonable doubt'. Must they be sure of the prisoner's guilt? The reply was, 'If you have reasonable doubt then you are not sure.' In such an event they would have to return a verdict of 'not guilty'. At 9.10 p.m., ten hours after retiring, they gave their verdict: 'Guilty'. No reasonable doubt, then. Asked if he had anything to say, Hanratty declared, 'I am innocent.' There was only one sentence.

On the evidence given at his trial, the case against James Hanratty was very thin. So thin, one wonders at a criminal justice system that can condemn someone to death, as opposed to, say, a life sentence, where at least if it is later discovered that there has been a miscarriage of justice the man or woman who is locked away can be released. You must be found 'guilty' or 'not guilty'. You cannot say 'guilty, but lock him up instead of hanging him in case we are mistaken.' The jury found Hanratty guilty after hearing the evidence. But they did not hear it all, as later events would show. Where, pray, is the justice in executing a person when the jury that convicts him does not hear all of the available evidence?

Hanratty's mother protested her son's innocence, but all mothers do. She was not with her son on that fateful night the previous August. Neither were any of his family or supporters. His last hope was a reprieve by the Home Secretary, to whom a petition of 23,000 signatures and 300 letters were submitted. There was no reprieve. On 3rd April Hanratty wrote a letter to his parents, praising their courage. He said, 'I am going to face up to it. I am going to be the son you can be proud of.' When the time came, he said, he would be thinking of them. 'Many a man would be glad to have the home you and dad gave to me,' he wrote.

At 8 a.m. the following morning James Hanratty was hanged in Bedford prison. He never confessed to the crime. But someone else did. On 22nd August the following year, the first anniversary of the murder, Peter Alphon visited Hanratty's parents, told them he had committed the crime and offered to pay them compensation. He confessed again, to a group of journalists in France. He confessed again on British television. He wrote to the Home Secretary, saying 'I killed Gregsten, the establishment murdered Hanratty.' Alphon was either a publicity freak or mad — or guilty.

Hanratty's Appeal

In 1999, over thirty-five years after James Hanratty was hanged, the case was referred by the Criminal Cases Review Commission (CCRC) to the Court of Appeal. The defence, and indeed the public as a whole, had been ill at ease with his conviction, so it was right to refer the case providing there was another ingredient to add to the many that had been trawled over the years. There was: DNA.

There were two material exhibits. The first was Valerie Storie's semen-stained knickers, the second the white handkerchief which was found wrapped around the murder weapon and boxes of ammunition, found on the number 36A bus in Peckham. At first they tried to extract a DNA profile from the knickers, but the test scientists applied failed. But DNA wasn't the only matter. The CCRC had discovered 'serious flaws' in the case. First there was the ESDA test (ElectroStatic Document Apparatus). This works like an ordinary photocopier, except that where a photocopier makes an image of a document, ESDA detects impressions of, say, handwriting from the overlying page. If you write on a notepad the impressions underneath, subject to the test, will show what you wrote.

In two of the police interviews with Hanratty, part of what he said had been changed — just as Hanratty had alleged in court. The police had discarded part of their original notes and substituted others, and now the pages below betrayed them. It may or may not have made a material difference to the outcome of the case, but if that was what the police were up to, one has to question the veracity of everything else they said or did. 'Kip' to 'sleep', of course, was one example.

There were lots of undisclosed documents, which the prosecution had not made the defence or the court aware of. They had chosen to submit only those that supported the prosecution case; those that did not they withheld. Some of these included statements regarding the alleged sighting of the Morris Minor and other important evidence.

This was not uncommon practice then. Today, the Crown Prosecution Service must be served with all documents, and they in turn must serve them on the defence as 'unused material'. In the 1960s, the police themselves were the prosecuting authority, and would be able to select documentary evidence to support their case.

These two factors played a major part in the case to have the conviction quashed. The defence said that had the jury been allowed to hear the 'hidden' evidence *at the time of the trial*, then an already tenuous case would have been thrown out. Remember: the case has to be proved 'beyond reasonable doubt'. Would there have been reasonable doubt if other witnesses, who did not support the prosecution case, had testified? We shall never know, as the jury in 1962 was not permitted to know. Given that the evidence that was presented was thin, 'not guilty' could have been the verdict. But then, the defence would seek the conviction to be quashed, even if by some means it was proved that Hanratty was, after all, guilty. It is their job to have their client acquitted.

Back to DNA. PCR (polymerase chain reaction) is a laboratory process used to copy parts of DNA in order to generate a DNA profile. They tested Valerie Storie's knickers and the white handkerchief and came up with DNA profiles suggesting the man who raped her also handled the gun used to shoot her and Michael Gregsten. But who was he? The Crown Prosecution Service sought the only means left to settle things once and for all: the authority to exhume James Hanratty's remains. The court agreed, and Hanratty's body was exhumed. From the remains scientists were able to obtain a DNA profile. They compared this to the DNA profile from the knickers and handkerchief and got a match. The defence, who truthfully believed Hanratty's innocence in my view, must have been dumbfounded. Considering the evidence, or lack of it, and particularly the chance 'find' of Hanratty's false name, J. Ryan, in the hotel register, the odds against finding the right man would have been overwhelmingly against. Yet there was a match. There was no doubt about it, the scientists said.

If, despite this, Hanratty was not guilty of the crime, there can be only two possible explanations. One, that Valerie Storie is a liar, and there is more to this than meets the eye, an unknown 'domestic' situation whereby she knew Hanratty all along and had sex with him and someone else was the killer; or two, that somehow contamination accounts for Hanratty's DNA coming up on the two exhibits.

The first is unlikely. Not even the defence have suggested that there is doubt about Valerie Storie's testimony, and be sure they will

---

The Verdict

They say detectives have a 'nose' for the truth. They do, some of the time. But not every time. They had a 'nose' in this case when they sought to put Peter Alphon in the dock. Maybe they were right. He could not be ruled out — until DNA ruled Hanratty in, if it did. Let there be no doubt: until the DNA evidence there was no proof 'beyond reasonable doubt' that James Hanratty was guilty. Even now, given the circumstances, and they are well documented, it is hard to believe that in the whole of London, J. Ryan, the name that fortuitously came up when detectives responded to a police circulation to hotels, should happen to be the man police wanted. Imagine if they had not — would the DNA profile have therefore had no match? Well, no, it wouldn't. The case would have been undetected. We must believe the scientists. If the DNA profile was from semen, Hanratty was probably guilty, at least of the rape. If not, or if its source is unknown, unidentifiable after 40 years, then there must be 'reasonable doubt' and his conviction should be quashed.

have looked. We must accept that she told the truth. As to contamination, it seems that during the trial, and maybe before and after it, all exhibits — Storie's clothing, the handkerchief, Hanratty's clothing — were often together, in the police station or in transit, possibly touching. But is the DNA from the knickers taken from whatever was left of *semen*, not fibres or Hanratty's hair or other body parts? If it is from semen, then the semen was Hanratty's. Hairs, etc., could have been deposited by contamination into the knickers. The scientists will say that had there been another party, if someone else was the killer, he too would have deposited DNA. But there was no other profile on these exhibits, only Hanratty's.

But was the DNA from semen? It is critical, surely. The samples were over 40 years old. Who is to say what decaying matter existed in the knickers and handkerchief — a tiny flake of skin or other body tissue, from which the DNA was extracted? We are getting into the world of science here; we need the scientists themselves, to explain. They do, and they say that contamination is 'unlikely'. But contamination of what: semen or something else? The exhibits had been in police possession for nearly forty years, lying on a shelf in a property store. What condition were they in by now? The Hanratty team may yet succeed in having the conviction quashed, if only on the grounds that he did not have a fair trial, and that he should not therefore have been convicted in the first place. That doesn't mean he didn't commit the crime. It means he should not have been convicted in 1962. If you were a member of a jury now, would you find him guilty?

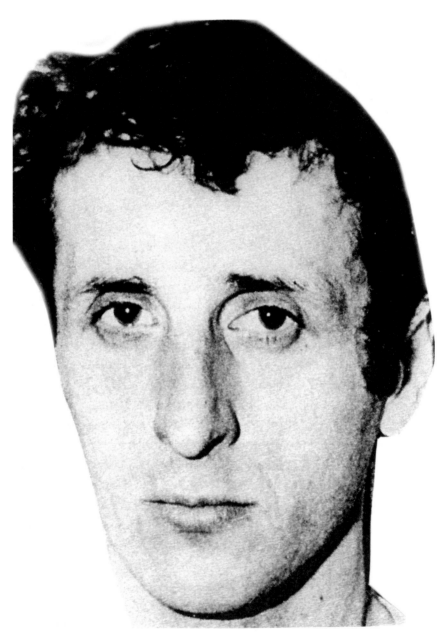

The Fox

Malcolm Fairley was given six life sentences

LINSLADE AND EDLESBOROUGH 1984–85

In the Lair of the Fox

'Bedford bobbies have been called away from policing miners' picket lines to join the massive hunt for the armed rapist known as The Fox'. So reported the Bedfordshire Times on 14th July, 1984, following a series of attacks in victims' homes in the 'Triangle of Fear', an area straddling the borders of three counties – Beds, Bucks and Herts. The Fox had struck terror into the hearts of homeowners in Leighton Buzzard, Tring and Cheddington, and scarcely was the ink on the newspapers dry than he was at it again. Little wonder that people were barring their doors and windows against night-time strikes by the unknown intruder who raped, assaulted and stole.

Malcolm Fairley, later identified as The Fox, opened his account of terror one April evening at the home of a 74-year-old widow at Linslade, Leighton Buzzard. His victim had retired to bed, then read for about an hour before turning out the light and settling down to sleep. But it wasn't long before she was disturbed by a shuffling sound to find a strange man in her bedroom. Fairley held a gloved hand across his face to avoid identification, sharply pulled back the bedclothes and indecently assaulted the woman. She resisted and he fled. Police may have considered this to be a one-off incident, as no other similar attacks were reported for a month. But The Fox struck again, this time in Cheddington, Bucks.

He entered an unoccupied house, and maybe his motive was

burglary, for he stole £300. But when he chanced upon a shotgun and cartridges he must have decided to stay, probably – if his later activities were anything to go by – to rape the householder when she returned. Instead, 'she' turned out to be a 35-year-old man who had been out for the evening with his girlfriend and who, on his return, found Fairley waiting, wearing a mask and pointing his own shotgun at him. Fairley tied his victim up and played some pornographic videos after which, possibly inspired by their sexual content, the man said he tried to bugger him, an allegation later refuted by Fairley. On leaving the house he buried the gun and was unable to find it again.

Three weeks later, Fairley, having committed a number of burglaries, struck again, when he broke into a house in Tring. He removed items from drawers and photographs from albums and again, fortuitously, he found a shotgun and cartridges. This time he would keep the gun, and shorten the barrel. From now on he would be armed on his night-time missions of crime, the next of which was two days later at Heath and Reach. It was the house of a married couple. They had gone out just before nine o'clock. Fairley, having got inside, set about removing light bulbs and made himself a 'lair' by moving furniture which he covered with blankets so that he could watch videos without being seen. Henceforth he became known as The Fox. He collected dressing gown cords and cut the telephone wires and fashioned an escape route before helping himself to food from the fridge and a cup of tea. When the occupants returned at 1.30 next morning Fairley fled, taking with him £130, an anorak and a packet of peanuts.

He didn't go far. Crossing the fields to a house in nearby Leighton Buzzard he entered whilst the occupants, another married couple, were asleep in bed. The first they knew of the intruder was the sight of a man wearing a balaclava style mask with holes for the eyes and carrying a sawn-off shotgun. He was visible in the glow of a night-light, kept on all night for the benefit of the couple's children. When the husband sat up in bed, Fairley shot him.

Shotgun pellets hit the husband in the hand, causing a nasty wound. Despite this, he chased Fairley from the house. The stolen anorak and peanuts from the previous entry that night were left behind. Later, when he was arrested, Fairley, referring to the shooting, told police, 'It just went off. I was shaking like a leaf. I hope I didn't harm him.' Since he had no experience with firearms, this was probably true. In fact, he was so shaken he committed no more offences for a month.

The police easily linked the crimes which, despite being committed in three counties, they calculated must be down to the same man. He was described as up to 6 feet tall, of slim, athletic build. They were very concerned about his conduct: collecting the cords of pyjamas and dressing gowns, ties and belts, which suggested he was looking to tie up victims and, if so, why he would do so. They opened an incident room at Dunstable police station and advised the public to lock all downstairs windows at night, and upstairs ones too, as the man had shown 'remarkable agility'. He was said to speak with a northern or possibly Geordie accent, and was probably left-handed. He was committing burglaries during daylight, but it was when he struck again at 5 a.m. on the morning of 6th July that Fairley, undeterred by publicity and the police operation, showed his true colours.

He broke into another house in Linslade, where a young married couple lay asleep in bed. They awoke to find The Fox pointing a shotgun at them. He ordered them to get up, and tied them up with clothing and shoe laces. He then indecently assaulted the wife who screamed, loud enough to scare off her assailant. As the police had suspected, his motives were sexual as well as theft. Four days later came another break-in, again at Linslade.

Again, a married couple were sleeping in their bed. Their two children were also asleep in the house. At gunpoint, the wife was ordered to tie up her husband, which she did, and then Fairley tied her up also. When he indecently assaulted her, the husband protested

147

Dunstable Police Station

and Fairley struck him with the gun, or his hand. He then raped the wife and left.

A wave of fear had by now swept through the area where Fairley was committing his crimes of burglary, assault and rape, his victims tied up at gunpoint and one of them actually shot. There were significant developments in the police investigation. In one, a senior officer made a desperate plea for Fairley to give himself up. 'I am sure you will realise we genuinely want to help you… I would agree to meet you so we can discuss the matter'. Whether it would be realistic for Fairley to consider the certainty of going to prison if he came forward was 'helping' him is doubtful, as would be the chances of 'discussing the matter'. The public were told, 'He could be Mr Nice Guy from next door, a Jekyll and Hyde type of character, with an evil side when offences are committed and a gentle side which is his everyday life'.

In another development, a computer was introduced into the police enquiry. Today, computers are an everyday tool of crime investigation (and most other things). In 1984 this was the dawn of a new age in Bedfordshire. Hitherto, a 'card index' system was universally used by police to record data, a system that had been exposed as inadequate, as in the Yorkshire Ripper case. Instant recall of accurate data is the important thing, along with the certainty that information will not be lost or misplaced once stored. This was just what the computer would provide, and officers from West Yorkshire were drafted in to help. But as a senior officer cautioned: the computer alone would not catch The Fox. 'It will not come up with the name and address of the criminal.' Indeed.

As the public barred their doors and nailed down their windows, and local hardware stores sold out of locks, the police took up covert surveillance. They hid in barns and houses, patrolled in unmarked cars, hoping The Fox would stumble into their waiting arms. A helicopter patrolled above, ready to swoop on suspected sightings, of which there were many. Even the Chief Constable came out on patrol. His advice to the public was that they should 'take care of their property, themselves and their neighbours' (shouldn't we always?). The police didn't get their man, but the crime rate plummeted. Any burglar mad enough to be out committing crime in the Triangle of Fear was risking arrest or being shot by angry members of the public, some of whom were armed themselves.

Meanwhile, Fairley kept his own observations, sometimes from the top of Ivinghoe Beacon, an excellent vantage point. He knew the footpaths, and after driving to selected locations would park his car well away from the scenes of his crimes. After each raid he buried the shotgun and other tools of his trade. Any police search of his property or car would have proved fruitless. He continued committing burglaries until, on 13th July, he raped again.

This time it was at Edlesborough, in a house occupied by three people: an 18-year-old woman and her 21-year-old boyfriend, and her 18-year-old brother. When the boyfriend got up to go to the toilet he saw The Fox, who was inside the house wearing his balaclava-style hood and carrying his shotgun. The young woman, hearing a noise, emerged from her bedroom and she too discovered The Fox. She, together with her boyfriend and brother, were taken at gunpoint to her bedroom and tied up with flex, the young men on the floor, she on her bed with a pillow case over her head. The Fox then calmly made himself a drink before returning to tear off the young woman's nightdress and rape her. Later, she would say, 'I thought I was going to die.'

Fairley ordered both men to also have intercourse with the woman, and when they failed he obliged them to simulate the act. He raped her again, before stealing various items including videotapes and then leaving the house. Later, at trial, the young woman would be commended for her 'courage and calmness'.

Eight burglaries later, this time in the Milton Keynes area, Fairley decided to go north to Peterlee, in County Durham, an area he knew very well. On the way, he committed another offence, which would lead to his demise.

His route that August night was by way of the M1 motorway, then the M18. He had the shotgun with him, but even so it may have been an act of spontaneity, perhaps his sexual urge now in full flow due to his success down south, that made him pull over on to the hard shoulder of the M18 and reverse into a wooded area where he left his car, then crossed the carriageways and headed on foot over the fields towards the lights of the South Yorkshire village of Brampton-en-le-Morthen. It was about three o'clock in the morning.

He arrived at the home of a married couple. Wearing a mask he had just made he entered and went to their bedroom where he woke them up, and tied them up. After searching the house he indecently assaulted the wife, silencing her husband's protests by thrusting the

Edlesborough Church

shotgun into his face. He then raped her. He had learned of the techniques of forensic examination of crime scenes, so he carefully washed and cut out a piece of bedding to prevent detection by blood grouping his semen. He returned to his car, on the way discarding mask and gloves and hiding the gun, and drove off. At Peterlee, no longer armed, he assaulted a Chinese girl in her home, and turned up at the address of a mother and her daughter where he had the door slammed in his face.

Fairley travelled south again. He committed more burglaries in the Milton Keynes area where, on 9th September, he entered a house where a woman lay asleep in bed, alone as her husband was at work. He lunged at her with a kitchen knife, and fled when she cried out. He needed the power given to him by the loaded shotgun he no longer possessed – but the game was up for Fairley.

Detectives investigating the offence in South Yorkshire had found The Fox's gloves and mask and the gun, and, significantly, the bag in which it had been carried, which had fingerprints on it. They would check out to be Malcolm Fairley's. The mask had been made by cutting off part of the leg of a boiler suit, or overalls. Then came a real breakthrough: in the little copse where Fairley had parked his car detectives found tyre marks and a broken twig with minute paint scrapings on it. Samples were taken, and when analysed the paint was found to be from a British Leyland car, harvest yellow colour.

There were thousands of Leyland cars. How could they possibly check out every one? The answer lay with a witness, a lorry driver, who had seen a car at the relevant time backing onto the hard shoulder of the motorway, but could not remember the make or colour. Under hypnosis he was able to recall that part of the car's registration plate bore a County Durham number. The South Yorkshire police had realised that the attacker at Brampton was almost certainly The Fox, and they passed all details to the incident room at Dunstable.

Detectives were sent routinely from the incident room at

Police step up hunt for 'Fox' after assaults on three young people

By Stewart Tendler, Crime Reporter

As police patrols searched property and watched the roads of a Chilterns village yesterday the armed man wanted for sexual attacks and burglary, nicknamed "The Fox", evaded their hunt, broke into a house and assaulted three young people. The police had been called to the village of Edlesborough on the Buckinghamshire/Bedfordshire border after a man reported an intruder escaping from his home.

Dozens of armed officers were brought into the area, some with dogs, but three hours later the man broke into a second house 500 yards away.

A girl aged 18 was raped twice and her brother, aged 17,

said: "I am fearful that the man will commit a murder."

Police advice to potential victims is to obey the man's demands – he never makes any conversation apart from giving orders in a soft northern accent – because of the risk of violence.

The man, about 5ft 9in tall, medium to stocky build, with brown curly hair, pullover and a balaclava helmet, made his first appearance in Earlesborough just after 11pm on Thursday.

Mr and Mrs Michael Jansen were asleep in their home when their pet cocker spaniel barked from downstairs. Mr Jansen, whose two children, a girl and a boy, were also asleep, went downstairs and reached the

may be someone whose family believes he goes to bed each night, when in fact he is out prowling.

Mr Prickett said that further offences were likely. The police have already urged the public to take care, and he acknowledged that local people were growing increasingly upset by the attacks.

The police operation is now a joint one between the Bedfordshire and Thames Valley forces and Bedfordshire police had withdrawn their officers from miners' picket line duty in Nottinghamshire.

Villagers were yesterday angry about the attacks on the three young people.

The Times, July 14 1984

Dunstable to trace and interview and eliminate owners of Leyland cars, harvest yellow colour. This would be a long, hard slog, whilst all the time The Fox was at large. There was always the chance he would find another gun. In any event, on 11th September, two detectives, dispatched to London, would come face to face with The Fox. In a reign of terror, where police had used computers, helicopters and hundreds of officers, taken over 15,000 samples of blood for testing and spent at least £200,000 in overtime payments, two plain clothes coppers, travelling by public transport, duly arrived at Oseney Crescent, Kentish Town, to interview Malcolm Fairley, the owner of an Austin Allegro, harvest yellow colour.

The car was outside Fairley's address. At once the detectives noticed scratch marks on it, and in the car they found overalls with part of a trouser-leg cut off. They also found a wrist watch in the car, and, recalling that part of the suspect's description was that he was probably left-handed, he was asked to put it on. Without hesitation he put the watch on to his right wrist, the action of a left-handed person. It was the end of the line for The Fox. But who exactly was Malcolm Fairley?

He was 32, a quiet, soft-spoken northerner and petty criminal – but not a man of violence until he terrorised the populace in the Triangle of Fear. He was born in Sunderland, the youngest of nine children. He got into trouble for theft and burglary, and married twice, with three children of the second marriage. For ten years he was in and out of prison, and in 1983 he moved to the Leighton Buzzard area to work as a labourer. Although he continued to commit crime, there were no sexual convictions recorded against him. It was when he chanced upon the shotgun and ammunition he

The Verdict

In February, 1985, Malcolm Fairley pleaded guilty at St Albans Crown Court to all offences charged. The crime count was 79, between March and September, 1984. Mitigating, defence counsel explained that he suffered from personal defects that were no fault of his own. Fairley was illiterate, innumerate and suffered from a speech defect. He'd had no father since he was 5 years old. He had no clear idea of right and wrong. 'These defects have rendered him more prone to commit offences of this nature than he would otherwise have been, and caused him to be susceptible to other extraordinary influences.' Counsel also had in mind the pornographic videos, adding that doctors and psychiatrists described Fairley as 'inadequate', meaning he had only a limited understanding of the wickedness of his acts. He had used 'minimum violence', and had not intended to use the shotgun. The judge said he had used it by carrying it, but point taken: he didn't intend to shoot anyone, that's what counsel meant.

changed from petty crook to monster. As he would explain himself, 'When I got the gun I felt I could get what I wanted.'

The police came out of this well. Sparing no effort when members of the public were living in fear of attack, officers from three south-east forces worked hard and professionally and with great determination to catch The Fox. They did well in South Yorkshire too, finding the tiny flecks of paint on the twig when Fairley parked on the motorway. The two detectives who arrested Fairley were commended by the judge, and rightly so.

O f his alleged indecent assault of the 35-year-old man in his home, Fairley had been 'experimenting', after what he had seen on pornographic videos. 'He thought it was something he might try,' explained counsel, adding that he was unaware he might be harming or upsetting any of his victims. When Fairley was asked by the police how he felt after he had raped a woman when wearing a mask and carrying a gun, Fairley replied, 'I thought she was good. She was great.' 'I meant did you feel sorry for her?' asked the interviewing policeman. 'I'm sorry I have been caught,' replied Fairley.

J ustice Caulfield told Fairley: 'There are degrees of wickedness beyond condemnatory description. There is no excuse for crimes which leave victims in utter terror and with lifelong frightening memories. You desecrated and defiled men and women in their own homes. You are a decadent advertisement for evil pornographers.' Fairley said he thought he needed treatment. He was probably right. There was plenty of time for it. He was given six life sentences.

Porn and Guns

Pornography and a loaded gun: a dangerous combination. At least in the case of Malcolm Fairley, who evidently was motivated by the former and having fortuitously acquired the latter set about terrorising people in their homes, motivated by sexual lust. As he said himself: 'When I got the gun I felt I could get what I wanted.'

But is pornography really a 'cause'? Can sexual titillation, however pornographic, influence someone sufficiently for he (or she) to act as Malcolm Fairley did? Maybe in 1984 they thought so. But today, with porn so readily available – magazines, the internet, even terrestrial t.v. – one wonders if it can. If porn was a factor in motivating sexual crime, by now we would have thousands of Fairleys. In the end, the question must be a subjective one: some people, a few, will react on having access to pornography, and others will commit sexual offences if they have the power to do so.

Before he carried a gun, Malcolm Fairley had no previous convictions for sexual crimes. But when he chanced on one in a 'routine' burglary, everything changed. His armed escapades may have been short-lived once the gun was no longer available to him, but then didn't he go and chance upon another, straight away, and then he went on to rape.

Guns, readily available in someone's house. This cannot be right, and the law to bar private use is a good law notwithstanding the majority of registered keepers of firearms were lawful, responsible people. As if the case of The Fox was not enough, think of Hungerford and Dunblane. Innocent people, many of them children, murdered by those who had lawful access to guns but were no longer in control of their minds. If there were fewer guns there would be fewer serious crimes.

HENCE, WHENCE AND THENCE

*"Criminals do not die by the hands of the law.
They die by the hands of other men."*

George Bernard Shaw

'You have been found guilty of the crime of wilful murder. The sentence of this court is that you be taken from hence to the prison whence you came, and that you be taken thence to a place of execution, there to be hanged by the neck until your body be dead... And may the Lord have mercy on your soul.'

To hang, or not to hang.

Let there be no doubt: the public would, if asked, vote for the restoration of the death penalty in this country. Again, let there be no doubt, they are not going to be asked. There would be no purpose in asking, for the power to restore it no longer lies with the elected government which sits in the now largely defunct British parliament. That said, would hanging murderers do any good? Would it deter them? Would it be justice?

Most murders are 'domestic', that is to say offender and victim are acquainted. Most are born of some spontaneous act, or are caused through drunkenness (which is no excuse). Few are premeditated. If they were going to have capital punishment, the 1957 Homicide Act seemed to get things about right. The Act abolished hanging for murder, save in the following circumstances:

157

Murder committed in the course of or furtherance of theft
Murder by shooting or explosion
Murder whilst resisting arrest or trying to escape
Murder of a police or prison officer
Two murders committed on separate occasions

At first glance this looks fair. It distinguishes between the spontaneous, unintended murder and cold-blooded murder in the course of crime — the armed robber, the terrorist, etc. On closer inspection it is flawed. The man who kills and steals one penny will hang; he who rapes and kills will not.

Hanging as a deterrent, then. If you kill you will hang. Will this prevent tragedies such as the murder of children, or murder by armed robbery? Who knows? When the death penalty existed people committed murder. When it was abolished people committed murder. Forget statistics; they are contrived, usually by the government to fashion some idea or other around them. Hanging as a suitable punishment? Each of us must hold our own views. Personally I consider putting a rope around someone's neck and pulling a lever so that they fall and suffocate is barbaric. OK, so murder is barbaric too. But there is another reason why hanging can never be reintroduced. Quite simply, the criminal justice system is a game of chance. Detectives investigate crime against the clock: if the prisoner isn't charged by such-and-such a time out he goes. The rules are weighted against those who give their best endeavours to seek the truth. Barristers pit their wits against each other, each seeking to win, which is not the same as seeking justice. In all this mishmash of rules and procedures remember: once someone is hanged, they cannot be brought back to life.

The jury in the William Bull case convicted a man without proof. As it happens, if his confessions are to be believed, they were right. They could just as easily have been wrong. Today, we can identify offenders (and victims) by fingerprints, blood grouping and DNA. Still there remains cause for doubt. One wrong conviction is one too

many. Hanging an innocent person is murder by the state. But the
law should be clear: life imprisonment may usually mean a number
of years imprisonment, with early release for good conduct if you are
no longer a threat; but for some crimes, and you know the crimes I
mean, it should mean for the remainder of an offender's life, never
to be released. Period.

The Last to Hang
Gwynne Owen Evans (above) and Peter Anthony Allen were hanged at the
same time, 8 a.m. on 13th August, 1964, at different locations, for the
murder of a man at Workington, Cumbria. Evans was hanged at Strangeways
prison, Manchester. Allen was hanged at Walton Prison, Liverpool. These
were the last lawful executions in this country.

Bibliography

A Study of Bedford Prison, 1660–1877, Eric Stockdale, 1977
The Trial of John Bunyan, The Folio Society
Where They Burnt the Town Hall Down, Dave Craddock, 1999
Crime in Bedfordshire 1660–1688, Evelyn Curtis
Oxford History of the Prison
History of Bedfordshire, Joyce Godber, 1969
Scandal in the Church: Dr Edward Drax Free, R.B. Outhwaite, 1977
Hanratty: the Final Verdict, Bob Woffinden, 1997

Newspapers
The Times
Bedfordshire Mercury and Huntingdon Express
The Bedfordshire Times
Beds & Bucks Observer
Leighton Buzzard Observer
Luton News
Dunstable Gazette
The Bedfordshire Times & Bedfordshire Independent
Bedfordshire Record
Post Echo

I wish to thank staff at Bedfordshire and Luton Archives and Record Service, County Hall, Bedford, and staff at Bedfordshire Libraries, who assisted with the research required to produce this book. Also others, too numerous to mention, who have helped in providing on-site information at locations around the county.

Special thanks to the Bedfordshire Times (information provided in their reporting of the Lucy Lowe, William Bull and Malcolm Fairley cases), and to Leighton Buzzard Observer (information on the Leslie Stone case).

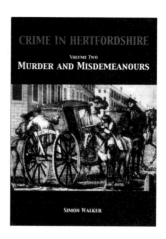

CRIME IN HERTFORDSHIRE
Volume One: Law and Disorder
Volume Two: Murder and Misdemeanours

Simon Walker

Volume One covers the history of law and order in Hertfordshire from the Anglo Saxon period to the middle of the twentieth century. Criminal law, the courts, the punishments and the means of enforcement have changed over the course of more than a thousand years, and the author traces those changes, illustrated with examples drawn from throughout Hertfordshire.

Volume Two is a collection of detailed accounts of crimes drawn from across the county, from 1602 to1939. Locations include Hatfield, Hemel Hempstead, Hoddesdon, Berkhamsted, St. Albans, Ware, Hitchin, Datchworth and Bishops Stortford – some of the incidents may be familiar, most will be new to the reader. The rape of Maria Wells by her own father, and the publicity given to her testimony in court, was a tragedy for all concerned. Did Jane Norcott commit suicide, or was it murder? Why did Mary Boddy stab five-year-old George Hitch?

But it is more than just a collection of bloody crime; it provides an insight into the way which many of our Hertfordshire forebears lived their lives.

BUCKINGHAMSHIRE MURDERS

Len Woodley

Thoroughly researched accounts of seventeen murders ranging across the old County of Buckinghamshire. Commencing from the early nineteenth century right up to modern times. Your will read about the Newton Longville shop-keeper murdered for a few shillings; the Dagnall killer; murders for no apparent reason at Buckingham and Denham; the unsolved murder of the canal man at Slough; love affairs that went tragically wrong at Burnham and Bourne End; a fatal ambush at Botolph Claydon; the Pole who wanted to be shot and a fellow country-man who escaped justice by fleeing to the Soviet Union.

There is the trooper who slew his girlfriend at Slough and hid the body under the mattress; the W.R.A.F girl who offered to baby-sit but met a killer instead; the bright young girl who went for a last walk down a country lane and the couple who were the victims of a man's obsession with himself!

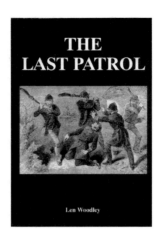

THE LAST PATROL
Policemen Killed on Duty while Serving in the Thames Valley

Len Woodley

This book details those Policemen who have been killed on duty by a criminal act within the area now covered by the Thames Valley Police – namely the counties of Berkshire, Buckinghamshire and Oxfordshire. It ranges from a Constable who, in the 1860s, died in Oxford just days after the formation of one of the constituent forces that made up the present-day Thames Valley Police and must surly be one of the shortest serving Policemen in this country, to the truly terrible day at Hungerford in the late 1980s, when so many people, including a traffic Constable, were murdered and others wounded in that picturesque Berkshire town. It encompasses Police officers encountering poachers, ejecting some drunken men from a public house, checking details of members of the visiting forces involved in a fracas in wartime England, attempting the apprehension of burglars and questioning some vicious, "stop at nothing" criminals over their behaviour in a motor car.

These police officers all started their day as normal, not one gave a thought to the possibility that he might be sent to a life-threatening job.

DEADLY DEEDS
A compilation of Buckinghamshire murder cases

Len Woodley

Included in this book are accounts of fourteen murders that have occurred within the County of Buckingham, plus one from central Europe. You will read about the Victorian 'Quaker' who, having escaped the gallows once, faced them again some years later; the country squire killed walking home from church; the gypsy who robbed and killed an old man, and the husband who shot his wife and her lover in one county, was tried in another and executed in yet another. A domestic dispute that went horribly wrong; a doctor murdered whilst out with her dog on an afternoon stroll and a Policeman who caught a killer as he patrolled his beat. A man who was killed in an argument over a dog; a teenager murdered by someone she thought she could trust and a young woman killed by an itinerant she had befriended. A Greenham Common woman, who accepted a lift in a car and was murdered because she did so and a young mother killed by a youth she allowed into her house.

The author was a Police officer for thirty years, serving in both uniform and C.I.D.

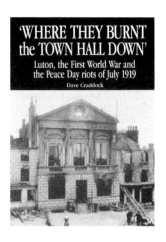

"WHERE THEY BURNT THE TOWN HALL DOWN"
Luton, The First World War
and the Peace Day riots of July 1919

Dave Craddock

The weekend of 19/20th July 1919 was arguably the most momentous in the history of Luton. What began as an afternoon of peace celebrations marking the end of the Great War turned into riots that had by the Sunday morning left the Town hall a smouldering, gutted ruin with the military in control of the town. Yet over the years, the story of the riots has been largely neglected.

Drawing broadly on contemporary documents, witness statements and newspaper reports, the book gives a blow-by-blow account of the riots, their aftermath and subsequent trials. The hostility between the Town Council and ex-servicemen's organisations in the preceding months is also covered extensively, as is the impact of the First World War on Luton.

Features of this book include informative appendices containing a wealth of information and over 50 illustrations.

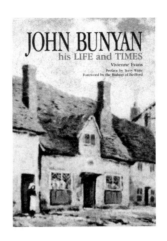

JOHN BUNYAN
His Life and Times

Vivienne Evans

Born to a humble family in the parish of Elstow near Bedford, John Bunyan (1628–1688) became one of the world's most widely read Christian writers – The Pilgrim's Progress eventually being translated into over two hundred languages.

This lively book traces the events of his life with its spiritual turmoil and long imprisonment, as well as discussing many of his writings. Clearly seeing Bunyan as a product of his time and place, it also explains the intriguing social, political and religious background of the turbulent seventeenth century.

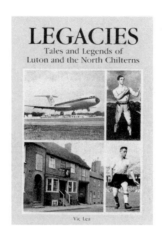

LEGACIES
Tales and Legends of Luton and the North Chilterns

Vic Lea

Vic Lea spent most of his lifetime researching and collecting famous and infamous historical tales of Bedfordshire and Hertfordshire. Following his best selling book, Echoes, here is a further choice of fascinating gleanings from his archives.

Recounted compulsively as only he could, Legacies offers twenty-five gripping sagas of yesteryear . . . bravery, murder, sport, riot, achievement, disaster, superstition, crime, devilry, transport, danger, intrigue . . . and many more such dramatic ingredients in an irresistible anthology of legacies from the past.

EXPLORING HISTORY ALL AROUND

Vivienne Evans

A handbook of local history, arranged as a series of routes to cover Bedfordshire and adjoining parts of Hertfordshire and Buckinghamshire. It is organised as two books in one. There are seven thematic sections full of fascinating historical detail and anecdotes for armchair reading. Also it is a perfect source of family days out as the book is organised as circular motoring/cycling explorations, highlighting attractions and landmarks. Also included is a background history to all the major towns in the area, plus dozens of villages, which will enhance your appreciation and understanding of the history that is all around you!

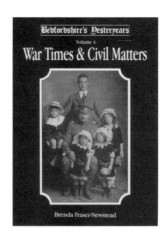

BEDFORDSHIRE'S YESTERYEARS
Volume 4
War Times & Civil Matters

Brenda Fraser-Newstead

Social history comes to life, first-hand and vivid, when seen through the eyes of those who experienced and shaped it.

The 'Bedfordshire's Yesteryears' series contains many privileged glimpses of a way of life that has changed radically. Here is the generation of two World Wars; here are the witnesses to countless technological and sociological transformations.

This volume highlights the angst of the Depression and the two World Wars, when the whole social fabric was disrupted but showed extraordinary resilience. It also traces another major feature of the twentieth century, namely the rapid development in all modes of transport – carriers and trams, airships and fire-engines, trains and automobiles.

Route marches, the General Strike, the Home Guard, the munitions factory, the Land Army, barrage balloons, evacuees, G.I. brides, the Specials, steam fire-engines, double-decker trams, the concert party – just a few of the evocative words that roll away the decades.